# *The Little Amazonian*

Miroslava Espinosa

Published by Richter Publishing LLC
http://richterpublishing.com/

Copyright © 2015 Miroslava Espinosa

Editors: Casey Cavanagh, Kelley Hutchison, Mandi Weems

Additional Contributors: Debbie Corson & Raquel Riesgo

Book Cover Designed by: Amitabha N.

ISBN: 0692531831
ISBN-13: 9780692531839

# *Reviews*

After reading Miroslava's book, I realized how much potential we have inside of us as human beings. Sometimes we try to find excuses for our limitations or failures, but at the end there is no excuse. It is up to us to find the energy not to just survive but to thrive through challenges of life.

Miroslava is the perfect example. Being born in very hard conditions, in a place where the only opportunity in life is to make it alive at the end of the day, this woman, found the strength to start another life, in another country, learning another language and unleashing her potential as human being.

In all her life, Miroslava proved to herself to be a fighter, not just in the warrior sense, but a fighter against the adversities of life. Never surrendering and never accepting mediocrity even when the odds seemed all against her.

I suggest this book to every person who wants to find inspiration in how to find new energy in challenging themselves, and at the same time want to discover how in some parts of the world human beings have to struggle every day for their basic needs.

When you feel you have it bad, just read this book, and you will feel better.

Gianluca Zanna
Host of Love Guns & Freedom Radio Show
www.LoveGunsFreedom.com

~

A beautiful story of trial and strength. Miro shows us by example as she demonstrates what can be accomplished through hard work, persistence, and determination. An inspiration to never give up on yourself. Never let your situation determine your future but rather be the keeper of your own destiny.

Truly an inspiration to all!

Emily Johnson Ingram

Wife, mother, motivational speaker, fitness model, World Champion Professional Natural bodybuilder, WNBF Professional Bodybuilder

# *Disclaimer*

This book is designed to provide entertainment only. This information is provided and sold with the knowledge that the publisher and author do not offer any legal or medical advice. In the case of a need for any such expertise consult with the appropriate professional. This book does not contain all information available on the subject. This book has not been created to be specific to any individual people or organizations' situation or needs. Reasonable efforts have been made to make this book as accurate as possible. However, there may be typographical and or content errors. Therefore, this book should serve only as a general guide and not as the ultimate source of subject information. This book contains information that might be dated or erroneous and is intended only to educate and entertain. The author and publisher shall have no liability or responsibility to any person or entity regarding any loss or damage incurred, or alleged to have incurred, directly or indirectly, by the information contained in this book or as a result of anyone acting or failing to act upon the information in this book. You hereby agree never to sue and to hold the author and publisher harmless from any and all claims arising out of the information contained in this book. You hereby agree to be bound by this disclaimer, covenant not to sue and release. You may return this book within the guarantee time period for a full refund. In the interest

# *Dedication*

I dedicate this book to the heart and soul of my existence ... My children, Monica Dalila Comstock, my six-year old little princess, and Christopher Bryan Taylor, my 16-year old son. Also, my mom, Maximina Hidalgo, who nurtured and loved me to no end, and my dad, Segundo Espinosa Montilla, my guiding light since I was a baby who taught me how to survive in the jungle, and how to fend for myself.

# *Acknowledgments*

I am forever grateful to Mr. Robert L. Chaney and his family for helping me with the rest of the funds for my book to become a reality. They have helped make my dreams come true, and the end result was more than worth the wait. Thank you, thank you!

# *Contents*

# *Introduction*

The desire to encourage, motivate, and inspire women around the world, especially those from third world countries, found its way onto these pages through my personal experience. More importantly to me, there are a lot of life lessons that other women and girls can learn from my life. I wanted to share these life stories with other women in hopes of connecting on a level worthy of their individual experiences. I wanted them to know that triumph can occur against insurmountable odds. Hardships can be turned into successes, and they can prevail as I have. I am living proof. I am a survivor, and they can be survivors, too.

Through these pages, I will show you firsthand what it's like to live through a times of scrounging for food and money, pedophilia, rape, gang rapes, murder, and death, as well as near-death experiences like a brain tumor, liver bleeding, and facing imminent threat with an assault rifle.

# *Childhood*

At nine months old, I crawled across the dirt floor in our tiny hut, over to a pot of boiling water on top a fire pit. My mom was cooking noodles for dinner, distracted by my brothers and sisters; she didn't see her baby on the floor inching closer to the red flames. The fire danced a crossed my inquisitive eyes. I grabbed the pot and tipped it over spilling the boiling hot water all over my chest. The hot noodles stuck to my little chest and I starting crying so loud everyone's attention was now on me. My mother ran over, gasping, "Oh my poor baby, what happened to you?!" She scraped the noodles off me and wiped up the scorching water. "We need to take her to the hospital!" She yelled to my father.

"No," he sternly responded. "She's a strong baby. She can heal herself. She'll be fine."

My mother said in disbelief, "She's only a baby, only nine months old. Look at her skin; she has serious burns. We need to go to the hospital."

"No." My father responded again. "If we go to the hospital, they will take her away from us." My mother agreed with him sadly and gathered some yuca plant instead. Cassava root (yuca) is rich in calcium and vitamin C and contains a nutritionally significant quantity of thiamine, riboflavin, and nicotinic acid. She sliced the yuca and placed is all over my burned skin. I started to calm down with the soothing vegetable working its magic.

Eventually, my body healed itself without having even one scar. If the boiling water had covered my face, I would have died. This was my first brush with death, but it would not be my last.

It was just the beginning of my journey as

*"The Little Amazonian."*

I was born deep within the forested Panamanian jungle in a small town called Nuevo Caimitillo. Our farm sat high on a hillside overlooking the Chagres River. A river historically known for its wealth in gold, proudly named "Castillo de Oro", the Golden Castile. The house we lived in resembled a Spanish-style hut, called a bohio. Its mud and thatch structure was built of reeds, red vines, straw, scattered foliage, and the clay soil nature provided for us. All at our fingertips for the taking. Our beds were framed using thick planks of wood, offering little comfort. Nights were restless. I'd lay inches above the ground, afraid of the critters that scampered beneath me and paralyzed by the fear of late night visitors. On occasion, snakes would climb the walls, while bats swooped in above us. The thought of either finding their way inside instigated many nightmares. The boa constrictor, known for its loud hiss and repeated strike when disturbed, packed a painful bite. I certainly did not want to be bitten or its next meal. The snake's earthy color, camouflaged by the dirt floor, made it easy to mistakenly step on. I prayed it would find its fill of mice, lizards, and whatnot outdoors, and that the bats would be eaten by the monkeys, owls, and falcons that desired them. On the unlucky nights when we had visitors, the nonvenomous boa attempted to swallow the bats, but often left hungry. The bats would sometimes linger, nibbling at our toes and ankles, leaving them bruised and bloodied. We would often awake in the morning with bloody legs and feet from where we were bitten by these vampire bats.

The absence of electricity and water in our home presented many challenges for my family. There was no water to drink or bathe in. Food was mostly gathered by hunting the densely forested jungle for rabbits, deer, and capybaras, or fishing the rivers for bass. Jobs were delegated in a traditional sense, where the boys hunted and fished, and the girls did the house chores such as laundry, cooking, dishes, etc. This hierarchy seemed totally unfair and quickly manifested the rebel in me. To my dad's dismay, I persistently begged him to teach me, as he taught my brothers. I hungered to be outdoors hunting and fishing. I wanted my dad to teach me how to shoot and become a skilled hunter like himself. I wanted the outdoors for the freedom and the challenges it presented.

"Daddy, let me go fishing with my brothers! Show me how to catch the big fishes in the river!" I would beg.

"No, no, no! You are a lady, and ladies belong in the house. The dishes are your job. Leave the fishing and hunting to us!" was his reply.

"No!" I would protest. "I don't want to stay inside and do the dishes! Dishes are no fun! I want to learn outside in the jungle ... with you!"

I'd find ways to sneak outside and be with my brothers. I'd disappear, leaving my mother frantic about my whereabouts. Abdiel, nicknamed Popeye, was two years older than me. He reluctantly resigned to the idea of a sister as his constant shadow. I followed him everywhere, desperately wanting to learn everything that my father had taught my brothers. I was intrigued by the sights and sounds of the jungle—tropical birds, wild games and rushing rivers. The deep, dark forest didn't scare me, as long as I had someone by my side.

There were seven girls, including me, and five boys in our family. Large by today's standards. I was the eighth of our 12 children. We had zero luxuries in our home; nature provided all the essentials we used. Daddy, our hero, was always searching for ways to fill our bellies. He was an agricultural man and a hunter. Some days he would go without food or sleep to ensure that we were cared for.

My mother was the nurturer of the family and always protecting us while our father was out hunting. Her small frame only stood 4 feet 11 inches tall, holding 105 pounds. A petite but strong woman, she gave birth to all 12 children in the jungle, without any medication.

All of my brothers and sisters attended first through sixth grade at the elementary school located a mile or so from our house. I was proud to be an honor student and constantly eager to learn. The journey to and from school was a bit rough. There were many poisonous snakes such as the bushmasters and Fer de lance (Equis) along the winding, sometimes treacherous path. Bushmasters are vipers that can grow to four meters (12 feet). The soldiers called them "two steps" because, in two steps, their lethal venom would begin to work its deadly affect. The Fer de lance or "Equis" as we usually called them because of the crossing patterns on the back of the snake resembling an X is venomous and very aggressive if disturbed. It can grow to two meters (about six feet) in length. The latter one was the most commonly founded in our early trips to school.

I vividly recall experiencing major separation anxiety on my first day of school. I laugh about it now. Granted, I was entering first grade and those feelings were thought to be normal, but they were devastating to me then. I begged my father not to leave me, grabbing his knees and holding on for dear life. "Don't leave me, Daddy!" I cried, my small body curled into a ball, shaking uncontrollably. A wide, reassuring smile crossed his face, as he looked from me to the teacher patiently standing by our side. He gently pried my hands free and said, "You're going to be okay." I wiped the tears from my eyes, determined to prove him right. He gave me a slight rub on the back, nudging me toward the teacher and walked out the door, not looking back.

My mother, of Kuna Indian and Chinese descent, originated from San Carlos, and my father, from

Santiago. My parents were chosen through an arranged marriage when my mom was a mere 16 years old, and my dad, 18. They moved in together two years later, but never officially legalized their vows. Hence, 54 years of togetherness with the absence of both papers and a ring! I never had the pleasure of meeting my grandparents. Their memory lived through pictures and stories that were shared. My grandfather looked exactly like my dad: dark skin, black hair and eyes, broad shoulders, and a height that challenged the trees in the forest. I often wondered if he was like him in other ways too: voice, mannerisms, and heart.

# The Apple does not Fall Far from the Tree

My father was an incredibly smart man. I remember him writing papers and speeches for General Omar Torrijos, a prominent Panamanian General, Commander of the Panamanian National Guard. Mr. Torrijos was best known for his part in the negotiation of the 1977 Torrijos-Carter Treaty that led to Panama's full sovereignty over the Panama Canal. The canal is of great importance to our country, and the world. It transports the wealth of nations: precious metals, jewels, commodities, and manufactured goods.

I'd like to think I inherited a healthy portion of my father's intellect and zest for life. He was a true believer in creating something out of nothing: leaving no stone unturned and embracing each and every life moment. My interest in public speaking can be attributed to him, which led to recognition and honors. I was chosen to speak in a competition about the provinces of our country and won second place out of several hundred students in various grades.

"You have done a good job, Miro," he boasted in front of family and friends. His daughter was his star. It felt wonderful to feel worthy of my father's love and admiration. I embraced the memory, holding it close to my heart for years to come. The recollection guided me toward future achievements and the possibility of obtaining whatever I wanted. I just needed to put my mind to it and work hard enough. Yes, I believed determination was another quality inherent of my father. Persistence, persistence, persistence!

I received a scholarship to middle school upon completion of sixth grade. It was a big deal! The scholarship awarded me the cost of books, materials, and uniforms. My uniform was a blue skirt, white shirt, white socks and black shoes. The clothes were nothing fancy, but graciously accepted. The value rested in the idea that it was earned through academic labor and free of financial cost to my family. I suppose it was the closest I'd get to stylish attire, especially a tom-girl growing up in the Panamanian jungle. And black shoes were easier to keep clean!

Many children were unable to complete school beyond the sixth grade, because they couldn't afford to go. The cost of books and uniforms were outrageous, and money was scarce and needed for necessities: food, clothing, shelter, etc. If only money grew on trees. The jungle would be the perfect place to get rich!

Unfortunately, education was placed further down the list of priorities. I couldn't imagine not placing it at the top. I loved learning. I wanted to know everything about everything there was to know!

My middle school years were harsh on me. I used to wake from slumber at the very early hour of three o'clock in the morning to prepare and travel the long distance. The dark sky tried to fool me into believing it was still the middle of the night. I'd have to pinch myself to rise for a new day, then quickly wash my face and dress. I'd walk the dusty trail in bare feet to minimize the amount of dirt on my socks and shoes. It was easier to try to wipe my feet clean of the sticky, red mud. My brother Popeye and sister Mireya would help guide the way by flashlight. Popeye would take the lead and Mireya the back. I took the middle. The three of us on lookout made it easier to spot intruders, especially deadly snakes.

Snakes were a constant worry, since they rested under the leaves from the trees along the trail. The important thing was to avoid them at all costs. Step around them, not on them! We knew which snakes to look out for, but the dark could make it difficult to identify them. Time wasted identifying gave the snake the upper hand. A defensive, aggressive snake would most likely strike. If it already devoured its prey, a food ball would be evident in its belly. It would look pregnant. The hunt and kill diluted the strength of the bite and the venom would be less toxic, but still poisonous. The fangs could pack a nasty, painful punch. We knew how to delay the poison using an anti-venom. Our dad had already taught us how to make it and what to use to create the potion in case he was not around if any of us got bitten. My brother had been bitten once and my sister three times – all by venomous snakes. I was scared to death and hoped the odds weren't in my favor of being next.

Thinking back on those treks to school, I'm reminded of all that I learned from my father and brothers. Even today, I am confident I could survive in the jungle, whether snakes, cats, or whatnot crossed my path. For example, I learned spear fishing as a little girl and frequently fished with my brothers and sister in our rivers. One of my first memories fishing involved something much bigger and worse than a little old fish.

"You get over here and drive the fish to the net!" My brother yelled at me.

"Me? Aren't you supposed to do that? Can I hold the net?"

He laughed. "No, no, no, no. You always say you want to learn. Now, it's your turn."

I started working the fish into the net. It wasn't as easy as it looked. The fish were big, smart, and fast. I always wanted to do what the boys did and not stay home cleaning the dishes, but this was harder than I thought!

Caught up in the moment and unaware of something foreign under water, I stepped on an alligator. Oh my goodness, an alligator! His back was all bumpy and hard. "Save me!"

The eight-foot gator took off with a single swish of its long, flat, jagged tail. Bubbles rose to the surface as it quickly descended the depths of the water, hopefully in search of fish or turtles, not to return to feed off of me.

Teeth or no teeth, the slap of its tail drew enough blood to cloud the water and the sight caused me to scream, "It got me, it got me! I'm bleeding bad! Help!"

"Stop crying like a baby! It's not much more than a scratch! Go clean it up and come back out here!" my brother said.

My father was furious with my brother after I relayed our story to him. I would've stayed out of harm's way if only my brother had done the job he was supposed to. *Hmmm*, I thought. *He must've pictured an angry alligator eating his little girl.*

It was a scary moment for a little girl, but it was also exhilarating! That gator didn't get this girl, no, not this time! All my sisters like doing the female chores, but not me. I always went against the grain and wanted to hang with the boys. This encounter with the alligator wasn't going to stop me anytime soon, either.

# *Jaguar*

Around the young age of six, my father sent my brother Omar and me into the jungle to set mango traps for capybaras. Omar was only four years old at the time. Yes, two little kids with a big responsibility. The capybara is considered the largest rodent in the world. Its size puts a rat to shame and it primarily comes out at night to feed. Night time was when my father preferred to hunt and kill it. Sometimes, the traps would attract other animals, such as deer or hogs.

Each of us had our sack of mangos. The sweet, yellowish-red fruit was heavy in our hands. I swung mine over my shoulder for better leverage. Off we went into the jungle to complete a job that usually took about two hours.

My bag was empty and my brother was close to using up all his fruit too. As, I stood watching him, a movement caught my eye. Goosebumps trickled down my spine and a cold sensation brushed the back of my neck. I felt someone or something watching us. I looked up and saw the flicker of a tail amongst the branches. Suddenly, I locked eyes with a rather large, spotted cat—a jaguar! Time stopped in that instant. I cloud hear nothing but my heart beat faster and louder in my ears. For a moment, I was mesmerized by the animal. The cat and I, just staring at each other, neither one making a move.

Her eyes were as dark as the night and her coat spotted and shiny. I thought, *How beautiful*. For a split second, I almost felt as if I could see deep into her soul. It was as if we were communicating on some other level. That she understood I was not there to harm her, and that we were not food. Suddenly, the animal pounced in my direction, scaring the life out of me. I could sense the strength in her graceful limbs as she went from branch to branch, working her way down. I swallowed hard. A jaguar's reputation wasn't friendly. I remember thinking that I, or we, were going to be eaten alive. Two small children devoured by one large mean and hungry cat.

The cat's attention then diverted to my brother. He continued putting out mangoes, oblivious to the animal stalking him. I whispered, "Omar, drop the mangoes. Walk very slowly. Let's get out of here."

"No. Daddy will be mad at me," he said. "I'm finishing the job. You're not getting me into trouble."

"Please, Omar. Let's go. Let's go to the river," I begged.

"Why?" he responded. I couldn't tell him we were being stalked by a jaguar. He would freak out and we would definitely get attacked.

I said sternly, "Drop your mangos and follow me slowly." The change in my voice made him follow my lead without any further questions.

The further we got from the cat, the less afraid I became. The thump in my chest slowed and my breathing returned to normal. I wiped the sweat from my hairline and under my nose. My brother and I wouldn't be dead meat. Not tonight.

Soon, we reached the river and jumped in because it was so hot outside. We swam and played in the cool waters while the threat of danger diminished. I completely forgot about the jaguar and what had happened a few hours prior. A few hours later, we headed home, tired from swimming, leaving the thought of mangoes, capybaras, and large, hungry cats behind.

We reached our village to find it in a state of panic. There was a jaguar cub on a cage, and someone or something was covered with some bloody blankets on the floor. "What happened?" I eagerly asked.

"A jaguar. It ate an old man! Tore him to shreds! They found a corpse in the jungle and there's blood everywhere!" a villager gasped.

"What?" I responded in disbelief. "I saw a jaguar in the jungle. I can't believe it didn't attack us. When we were off setting the mango traps, I also saw an old man walking on the trail further down off to the side after we spotted the jaguar. Is that the man who got killed?"

"Yes, but he is dead now. We found his corpse and a jaguar eating his remains. We killed the animal and that is when we saw the cub hiding in the bushes. So we caught him, placed it in a cage, and brought him back to the village. There he is now," the villager said, pointing to the cub.

I couldn't believe my ears. It took me a moment to gather my wits before I could speak.

"We saw a big jaguar over there a short time ago! It looked me in the eyes, then disappeared!" I said, pointing a shaky finger in the direction we had come from, but I didn't see a cub.

Why didn't the jaguar attack us? Why the old man? I closed my eyes tight, trying hard to erase the images invading my head: the old man being torn to pieces by the big cat. I could hear screams as flesh was being stripped from his body. The blood oozed from the wounds, as each organ was torn from their cavity and devoured with an incredibly evil force. The withered man's frame crunched in the cat's powerful jaws and the snap of skin repeatedly echoed. I felt sick. I dropped to my knees, forcing the bile back in my throat before swallowing hard.

"Stop! Stop!" I yelled, desperately trying to get the images to cease, the film reel to pause.

Yet, why did the cat spare us? Was she just looking for food for her baby? Could the cat have sensed that we were just children and decided to spare us and take the old man instead? A sort of law of the jungle, where the old ones are killed to feed the little ones? Well, in a sense, my brother and I survived being eaten by a jaguar, which was a scary, scary thought. I cried for the old man.

# *Beehive*

We had many dogs growing up, but Orejas was my favorite. A disease of sorts riddled his body, which left him practically bald. Only a few patches of dark hair here and there covered him. We would joke that he was like a snake shedding its skin. The difference being, he never grew a shiny new coat. Hairless or not, he was our dog and followed us wherever we'd go. One day he came running home, howling in discomfort.

"What's wrong, boy?" I asked, puzzled by his behavior. He ran in circles around me, nipping at his own flesh and drawing attention to several markings on his back.

I knelt down, trying to get a closer look at the spots. His tan coloring had morphed into a sort of reddish brown.

"Bee stings!" I shrieked. "Poor Orejas. Poor, boy! There are so many. I've lost count!"

My father walked over to me and Orejas. "What's wrong with him? Is the dog sick?"

"Bees!" I cried, pointing to the marks on the dog's back.

"Ah! I must pee on him," he said. "Urine is a cure all for bee stings." My father started to unzip his pants, then stopped. "No, wait. Let's try balsamino."

The balasimno vine grows along the banks of the river. The leaves are part of the jungle pharmacy. We crushed them for their medicinal properties. In this case, we used it to treat the bee stings on our poor dog.

Relieved, I watched him gather the wild weed which is abundant on the banks of our rivers. He crushed up a healthy handful, methodically lathering it over the dog's back and belly. Within minutes, the healing began. Orejas' coloring returned to somewhat normal. He ran off, tail wagging. Amazing!

I yanked Popeye out into the jungle against his will to find the attackers and get revenge.

Eyes in the air, we watched a flurry of activity in the mango trees. A handful of bees were circling the biggest hive I had ever seen.

"Oh my gosh! It's huge!" I screamed, hands flailing in the air. "I bet they're the bees that stung Orejas! Popeye, you must destroy it!"

Taking a step backward, then two, Popeye said, "I don't think that is such a good idea," he stood shaking his head. "Look at the size of it! It's a monster! I'm not touching it!"

"It can't stay! Popeye, you have to get it down! Hurry, climb the tree! I'll get our slingshots!"

"No, wait! Stay here! I don't want you hitting the hive when I'm up there."

Popeye scurried up the mango tree, reaching for the hive. With a stick, he starting smacking it, causing a frenzy of bees to emerge. Angrily, they circled the outskirts of the hive and him.

"Shoo!" he yelled, swatting at them with his clenched fist. "Get out of here! Darn bees!"

The sudden movement caused him to lose his balance. He shimmied down the tree, scraping the rough bark as he made his way clumsily to the ground, bees covering him from head to toe.

"Run, Popeye, run!" I yelled, racing for the river. Bees darted everywhere. I could hear the loud buzzing in both ears and Popeye's footsteps close on my heels. I grabbed a piece of bamboo, tearing it from its stalk, and dove into the water. Safely underneath, I used the bamboo to gulp in tiny bits of air. I hid beneath the surface, terrified to emerge. I realized that they were killer bees and famous for their excessive defensiveness of their hives. They were not going to let us off easy.

Popeye grabbed a canoe lying on the riverbank, flipped it over, and huddled underneath it. I was floating down the river with the current moving farther away from the bees. He was still stuck under the safety of the canoe, yet it didn't fool the bees. The swarmed over top of it, waiting for him to emerge.

Finally, I edged myself toward the shore and slowly crawled out on all fours. Lying low, I scanned the area, half expecting to be bombarded by another onslaught of angry bees. The air was still, yet heavy and thick from the humidity. A lone rabbit scampered across the clearing, fading into the brush. Standing, I shook the water from my hair and careful not to scrape the swollen bumps that has emerged from the bee stings.

I looked down the river where Popeye was still under the canoe stuck on the river bed. I laughed at him and he cried for me to help him. I told him he needed to distract the bees and move away from their swarm. In order to help him I got some plastic bags and a stick. I went back to the river where he was trapped and wrapped the bags around my body to avoid more bee stings. I slowly reached out and took the stick to push the canoe into the current of the river.

The canoe started moving downstream, but the bees followed him persistently. Finally, he dove deep underwater and swam out from under the canoe, holding his breath until he was far enough away in the opposite direction. The killer bees still swarmed the boat and followed it far away from us.

We were thankful that neither one of us had an allergy to the stings. My arms and legs were covered. Some marks looked like they were blending into one shape, not two. There were an awful lot, swollen and red. They itched! And they hurt, too!

"You are going to pay for this!" my brother yelled.

"You're okay. We're okay." I giggled.

We kept our distance as we passed the remaining hive dangling high in the mango tree. I held my breath, feet as light as a feather, trying not to disturb the bees. Hopeful they'd remain still and oblivious to our closeness, my brother and I walked side by side, heads turned upwards in unison. The insides of the hive spilled out, exposing layers of silky skin and what looked like an army of bees. I shivered at the sight. We headed home, knowing that's exactly where we wanted the hive to stay: high up, out of reach, and undisturbed.

"Where have you been?" my father asked, looking us up and down, surveying our red, swollen bodies.

"We fought off a swarm of angry bees!" I painfully said. "The river saved us! We ran into the water for cover, came out and the bees were gone. Half the hive is still up in the tree, but the bees are sleeping now."

"I don't think the bees are sleeping," my father said, eyes fixed on mine. "Come with me, the two of you. I'm going to teach you how to kill the bees, once and for all!" My brother and I looked at each other, shrugged and ran to catch up.

My father used "nidos de termitas" (termite nests) to smoke out the bees. When set on fire, the termite nest will burn for hours, releasing a thick smoke until it's burnt to ashes. My father placed the nest on a stick, lit the corner on fire, climbed the tree next to the hive, and quickly placed it inside the remains of the killer bees home. Big clouds of black smoke filled the air and bees start flying out dazed and confused, not sure who or what is attacking them. I concentrated on breathing in slowly through my nose, afraid to open my mouth and fill my lungs with the nasty air.

Regardless, my eyes burned, tears streamed down my face, and my throat felt painfully raw. I was happy we were able to knock down the rest of the hive. My dad beat the charcoaled remains with a stick until it showed no signs of life. Happily, we threw the tattered pieces into the brush, watching it disappear far, far away from us and the mango tree branch. Our beloved family dog and our family would be safe from now on.

# *Mustang*

My eighth birthday presented itself with many new and interesting things, especially in my imagination. Deliver me the biggest, brightest, most colorful balloons and confetti! Bake me the creamiest chocolate on chocolate cake with an extra dash of sprinkles and offer me up the biggest slice! Shower me with ribbons, bows, and boxes galore! Stuff them full of goodies and spread them out all over the floor!

"How I wish such a wish could be simple and true!"
I sang to the heavens, humming a tune.

I skipped about, singing my birthday song and
feeling a bit glum. I knew wishes were just a want that
would never come true. There weren't birthday
presents or cake for my brothers and sisters. I sighed at
the thought, but didn't lose hope. Maybe this year, that
would change.

My dad had always been a horseman. He raised
one mare, one stallion, and two foals. When the mare
birthed a male, I was over-the-top happy. I'd get the
chance to see him grow into adulthood; to transform
from a tiny, delicate being into one of great stature and
strength. It was so exciting! For the next years of the
foal's life, I bathed and brushed him, and brought him
fresh water. We developed a special bond, an
undeniable trust not to be broken.

I had one wish, the wish that kept me up at night
dreaming of lightning speed, grace, and beauty. I
wished to ride my father's horse. To saddle its velocity
and agility, bareback. To jump on and ride with wild
abandonment!

"I want the foal for my birthday, Daddy! Oh, how I
want him!" I wanted the young black horse named
Potro. The name means Mustang in English – a free-
roaming, wild horse. That foal was not a baby anymore

and he was now close to one ton of muscles weight and giant in comparison to my 4'10" frame, and weighed 85-90 pounds.

"No," he said, simple and firm. "You are a crazy girl! The horse isn't tame. He's far too spirited and strong. His handler needs to break him before he'd be of any use to you." In a tone defying defeat, I said, "I can tame him myself. He loves me! Really, I can! Oh, Daddy, give me a chance!"

"No, you can't. You'd fall off and be trampled, crushed into the earth! Poof! You'd be gone!" he said.

"Oh, Daddy! Please, please let me try!" I begged.

Breathless, I cornered him in the pen, showering him with overzealous enthusiasm. He shook his head back and forth.

"This is not something your mother would approve of, either. But, I will let the horse teach you a lesson. Hopefully, he doesn't break your neck when he bucks you off."

My eyes bulged to the sized of saucers. "I can try?"

With a skip in my step, I placed a rope around Potro's neck and led him to the river. He stayed on the path, straight and narrow, until we reached the water's edge.

"Whoa boy! Down, down! Good boy." I pulled firmly on the rope and stroked his neck and jawline. He danced a dance and shot right into the water and right back out again. I was thinking he must've been encouraged by the coolness of the river, but afraid of its swiftness. The river was a good, perfect teaching ground and I was determined to conquer him at all costs. Once I got Potro shoulder deep in water, I mounted him and he repeatedly bucked me off into the river. Not put off by his power, I continued to mount him many times with the same results.

I mounted Potro for the umpteenth time. My body tired and sore, "Do it for me, boy" I whispered. Somehow, horse and rider connected or maybe he was just too tired to buck me off one more time. The seconds that followed were supreme.

I exited the river on his back, bareback, holding tight to his mane. Finally, I had conquered Potro and he was mine. From that day forward horse and girl became one.

"Did you know that the Chagres River feeds into two oceans? Did you know that five of the world's seven sea turtles can be seen at different times throughout the year in Panama, and bats can see with their ears?" I'd go on and on reciting what I'd learned that day at school, careful not to leave anything out. The space was a mixture of serenity and acceptance. My horse loved me and I loved him back. I could tell Potro anything!

My horse was tame and broken! Amazing! Well, one girl and one girl only could ride him freely. Others were tempted, but deterred by his spirited energy. Not my father, unfortunately. He wouldn't have a daughter undermine him with more sophisticated horsemanship than he. My mother pleaded with him not to do it. She warned him, "Segundo, you know that horse is Miro's, and he's going to buck you off! Crazy horse! Crazy you!"

Her words floated in the air, useless. At the time, I didn't realize my father had been drinking moonshine whiskey. *Seco Herrerano* we called it. He drank the hard stuff. Bravery in a bottle, as my mother would say. He'd had plenty of *Seco* to give him the courage to ride and plenty for my mother to worry about.

"It's about time someone else rode him," my father stated, tipping his hat. He didn't see it as reckless. So, down by the river we went. He mounted my horse, using a large rock as a springboard, *Seco* in one hand and the reins in the other. The first few seconds were a success, and then all went downhill. An approaching truck caught Potro's attention, causing him to arch his back.

"Heeey! Wait a minute, boy!" my father yelled, holding on tight to the horse's reins.

I had trained Potro to race cars. The word "Go!" signaled action. Sometimes, the sight or sound of a car could set him into motion. Unfortunately, my father was unaware of this. Low and behold, the appearance of a truck started the race. Potro darted at the sound of the truck's engine. I screamed, "Daddy, hold on! Hold on tight!" I jumped up and down. Potro darted ahead. He sped quicker than the four wheels. I prayed that horse and man would remain one. If mother could see HIM now! God save the both of us! He bounced up and down on his back, arms up in the air still holding his *Seco.*

They reached the end of the street and Potro stopped dead in his tracks. To him, he had won the race and now it was over. My father in his drunken stupor was thrown over top and landed in the dirt right on his butt, alcohol bottle intact, and hat on his head! I ran, cursing myself for having trained my horse to race cars. Secretly, I acknowledged Potro the winner. My father sat on the ground, fire in his eyes.

"Are you okay, Daddy?" I mumbled underneath my breath, while trying to hold back the giggles as it was amusing. No one can ride my horse but me. My father mumbled some words and got up look at Potro and I knew he wasn't physically injured, but his ego was. I can see it on my dad's eyes that he was debating what should he do to my mustang. After a few minutes that seemed like hours, he looked back at me and told me

"Take your horse away from me before I ride him again." I immediately took Potro back to his feeding grounds by the river.

I spent the latter part of the afternoon seeking shade under the dense, green canopy not far from Potro's pen. I went through the events in my mind and smiled to myself. My father was pissed, but I had trained my horse to race and win!

# *Popeye My Brother*

My brother Popeye was two years older than I, and he regretted that I was his shadow. We had developed this love-hate relationship because I looked up to him to emulate everything that my father couldn't teach me. So, I copied everything he did, every move he made.

On my eighth birthday, I had received some candy as a gift. Popeye saw me eating them and wanted to have some. I told him no, because they were given to me for my birthday, plus I had almost eaten them all.

Candies, goodies, and cakes were luxuries our poor family didn't get that often. So, of course I was not going to share with him, especially because he was always picking on me and unintentionally hurting me. So, I told him no, and I could see his face change, but at the moment I didn't care. I was savoring every bit of these goodies.

Later on, my brother approached me, carrying a box and wearing a mischievous grin.

"Whatcha doin' sissy?" he said.

"Oh, nothing," I said through a big yawn. "What's in the box?"

He played with the box, pausing before answering the question. "There's something in the box for you, a birthday present. But you have to put your hand in to get it."

"But you don't get me presents," I said nervously.

"I'm nice now," he smiled mischievously.

Thinking to myself, *Is it a puppy, a kitten?* I could hear scratching sounds from inside the box. I slipped my hand into the box, feeling around for hair, fur or a tiny lick. "Ouch!" I spat, pulling my hand out and nearly losing my balance. I looked at my finger and saw a baby alligator attached to it. I shook my hand, trying to get it off my finger.

I screamed in pain, blood on my fingers. Baby alligators have sharp teeth and this one got a chunk of my finger. I started crying and told him that I was going to get him for this. He better watch his back from now on!

Popeye rolled on the ground, clutching his stomach and choking with laughter. The echo sent a flutter of birds into flight and feathers trickled down like a wind-swept rain. "You should see your face!" he howled, overcome by hysterics.

It wasn't the first time he'd infuriated me, and it wasn't the last time I got even. I waited for a day or two after the alligator incident and plotted my revenge.

On the way home from school, we passed "the mean dog's house". This was the neighbor's dog who would bark and attack anything that would come close to him. He was such a nuisance to everyone in the village. The owner didn't care of him and never had him tied up. When we walked by, I had an idea and set my plan into action. I threw a stone at the sleeping dog, sure to hit it squarely on the head. Quickly, the dog jumped up on all fours, growling. My brother was front and center, and the dog eyed him as the attacker.

An evil smile grew on my face as I watched him run toward my brother.

"What the heck!" my brother yelled, sprinting for safety.

"Run faster!" I screamed, running behind with a stick in my hand. The dog got a hold of my brother's ankle and bit down hard. He screamed so loud in pain. Popeye fell to the ground. I hit the dog with my stick, after watching for a bit. Then I started yelling the owner's name and he finally came outside.

A sharp whistle sounded and the dog immediately turned and ran in the direction of the sound. "You jerk! I could've been killed!" Popeye cried.

I felt a little bad, but I had previously warned him I was going to get him back for the birthday surprise.

My brother was in pain all night long. His wounds got worse and his ankle swelled up big. I felt guilty as I probably overdid it this time. I grew angrier at the dog and decided I needed to get rid of him since he'd hurt other people in the past as well. That night, I plotted a strategy to make the dog disappear.

I returned the next day to execute the plan. My father had taught me how to use poison dart frogs to hunt. It was common practice to use it in the spears and darts to kill animals while hunting. I grabbed a portion of a tree that looks similar to cotton balls, and dabbed some poison on to it for safekeeping. When I found the dog scavenging for food, I carefully pulled out a wadded-up piece of bread and soaked in a mixture of toxic frog secretions. I threw the poisoned portion of bread on the ground near the dog.

The canine sniffed it out and immediately gobbled it up. Within minutes, the dog foamed at the mouth, choked, and took its last breath. My eyes got big as I watched him die. I didn't feel sorry for the nasty dog one bit. I wanted him to pay for what he did to my brother and to others. He was only supposed to chase and scare him, not hurt Popeye.

Now, with a dead dog in my presence, I had to get rid of the evidence. So, I dragged the dog all the way down to the banks of the river where the caimans and alligators had their home. I splashed the water first to make sure they would come when they heard the noise of the carcass hitting the water. The splash startled a group of alligators sunning on the opposite side. I heard a noisy swish of tails and a rustle in the leaves as they made their way to the floating dog. I ran to the safety of the banks and from there, watched the alligators have their snack for the day. I smiled to myself, dusted off my hands, and headed back home.

# *My Father's Accident*

"Stop crying, Mama! Please stop! He's going to live!"

My father had taken a gunshot wound to the chest. My oldest brother, Roberto, had pulled the trigger. They were out hunting, deep in the thick of the jungle, far from our home. Night was closing in fast. The last slivers of daylight illuminated the forest floor, barely lighting the ground or surroundings.

"I didn't see him!" wailed Roberto, wiping the tears with the back of his hand. Dirt smeared the dampness, leaving skids across his face. "I thought it was a deer, but it wasn't! It was too late! The gun went off. I couldn't stop it! I shot Papa!"

My father lay on the forest floor, fighting for his life. Blood drenched his white shirt. A pool formed around him, gradually seeping into the dry earth, leaving it caked and cracked.

"Roberto, listen to me." The words were barely audible. Roberto leaned closer, placing his ear against the side of his father's face. He couldn't comprehend what he was saying. The words were all jumbled.

"What Papa? What are you trying to tell me? I don't understand!" Roberto cried.

"You must remain calm, Roberto, and go for help." My father's words were a whisper.

"But Papa! I can't leave you here dying! I can't!" he cried.

My father clutched the Christ-like image dangling from a chain on his throat. He rubbed his thumb and forefinger up the glass base. "You must go, Roberto, or I will die." My father closed his eyes and didn't speak another word.

Roberto ran, blind to the razor-like scratches lashing out against his arms and face from the black palm trees. Adrenaline seized his senses. Fear drove him on. He had to get home. He had to get help to his father. A zillion things rushed through his mind, but mostly the sight of his father's bloodied form laying listless on the ground and his chest blown wide-open. Bits of frayed flesh encompassed the wound. Its edges heavily clotted in blood. The boom rang over and over again in his head. The gun fired, kicking him backward. The bullet tore through his father's chest with the shrapnel, scattering two-fold. It left pieces of flesh everywhere, rendering his father's upper body unrecognizable. The scene was horrific.

"It was dark, Mama! I thought there was a deer by the river, not Papa!" My mother was in a state of hysteria. She kept wringing the towel in her hand. The tears flowed and her shoulders hunched, causing her to look years beyond her age.

"Your father! We can't survive without your father!" The room stood in silence. My father's death would crush my mother and devastate our family.

"He's not dead, Mama! He's alive. He sent me to get help!" Roberto cried.

"He's alive, Roberto?" Her eyes widened in disbelief.

"Yes! He's alive, Mama! He told me to come get help! He said he'd wait for us! He'll be okay!" he said hurriedly.

"Hurry then! You must make your way to town and bring help! Go!" Mama yelled.

My brother went to town and brought six older men, all friends of my father, with him to try to help him out of the forest and carry his body to the hospital before it was too late. They were so worried thinking that by the time they arrived he would be dead, that they got there by running through the jungle in only four hours, when at normal pace it would have taken them at least six hours. The hammock carried the barely-breathing shell of my father to the hospital. I didn't see him for three months. The doctors removed forty-five pellets from his upper torso, two of which sat a mere millimeter from the heart, and one lodged directly in it. The doctors felt that the one lodged in the heart could safely stay. With the exception of a single pellet, mere millimeters saved his life.

My mother, who was very pregnant at the time, rode the bus to the hospital each day to visit my father.

She walked into town to catch the bus, or what we called the transport truck, and made her way to his side. Sometimes, she traveled in and didn't travel back. Those nights in particular, I kneeled by my bedside, praying for my father's recovery and my mother's strength. My older brothers remained at home, taking care of me and all my little brothers and sisters while my mom was with my dad in the hospital. Big brothers or not, I remember I didn't think I needed a babysitter back then.

Eventually, my father was released from the hospital and I recall him coming back very skinny, very frail, and I wondered to myself how he'd managed to stay alive after so many months there. But he was back now, and our family was one again.

# The Cashew Tree

"I'm hungry!" I said, waiting for someone to acknowledge me.

"Me, too!" said Popeye. "You want to get some marañon?" Marañon is an oval or pear-shaped structure, that develops from the pedicel and the receptacle of the cashew flower. It ripens into a yellow and/or red structure about 5–11 cm long. The pulp of the cashew apple is very juicy. The cashew is the seed. "Oh, yes! Yummy in my tummy!" I said, licking my lips.

"Follow me! " He said, taking off. "First one to the tree gets all the nuts! "

Popeye made it to the tree first.

"No fair!" I told him. "Your legs are longer than mine!"

Up he went, reaching quickly from branch to branch. I scurried up, trying my best to catch him.

"I'm a monkey! Monkeys climb faster than brothers!" I felt the weak branch give out under my footing. I tried hanging on, but couldn't hold my weight. I fell for three stories.

I woke up in my bed six hours later. The height of the fall had knocked me unconscious. I had a splitting headache and fever.

"Miro, your eyes don't look right," my mother said when she saw that my eyes were rolling back into my head. "Do you remember what happened to you, little one?" she asked, worry furrowing her brow.

I didn't remember anything at all. I was only aware of the burning fever and a terrible headache that was killing me.

"You fell from the cashew tree yesterday, Miro... I thought I'd lost you, my little girl," said my mom. My father was not around when the accident happened, but when I woke up six hours later he was back and very upset at me and my brother. Of course, he didn't tell me at that time what he was thinking, although I could tell he was really upset. Maybe he didn't say anything to me because he knew I'd already learned my lesson. For the next few days, I remained in bed, and my dad was by my side taking care of me and giving me aspirin.

"Take these pills, Miro," he said. For him, aspirin was the miracle pill. He liked to take aspirin for everything and gave it to us whenever we were feeling sick. "Your head will feel better," said my dad, handing me the small pills and a glass of water. I swallowed them, feeling the tablets scrape my insides while going down.

After a few days in bed with a fever and endless headaches, I was not getting any better. My oldest sister, Guadalupe, who lived in Panama City, was getting really worried about me and told my mom to bring me to the hospital. We didn't have money to pay for the fees, but Guadalupe pulled money out of her savings and was ready to pay for it.

We took the long trek to the city so I could get my head examined. I had a CAT scan performed that showed a rather prominent blood clot. This was the culprit that had mercilessly pounded the walls of my skull for the days. My sister and my mom asked the neurologist what was next, and he told them basically to put me on bed rest, monitor me closely, and to up my dose of aspirin. *Hmmm, I thought. Daddy's cure-all is a cure.*

The doctor also told my sister and mom to bring me back in a couple months to get another CAT scan, to make sure the blood clot was gone and not growing in size. But since we didn't have the means to pay for it, my family never took me back. So, I was left not knowing if it was still there.

What I didn't know at the time was that this one single fall would have a major impact on the rest of my life.

# *The Law of the Jungle*

Everything happened one day when I was returning home after attending my classes at the junior high school in the city. During this time, I had to wake up very early in the morning and go to sleep very early, too. If I missed my bus, I was in trouble, big trouble. I had no opportunity to stay with anybody in the city, since I was not very familiar with it and didn't know anyone there. I was getting up daily at three o'clock in the morning to walk barefoot to the bus stop so I could get to school on time; and then coming back to the farm late in the evening, so tired and exhausted that I couldn't think of anything other than getting ready to go to bed. That was my routine for three years, going from home to school and from school back home. I never wandered anywhere around the city; everything was new to me and I was scared of going around on my own.

We had projects at the school and the teachers grouped us together. Often my classmates asked me if they could come to my home to finish our homework there and I was always looking for excuses to not bring them to the farm. I felt so embarrassed of telling them that I was living in the jungle. *They will never understand it,* I thought, and so I had very few friends in school. One of my few girlfriends was Gloria, she was the only one who knew where I lived and understood me. But my behavior, school supplies, and my worn out uniforms ultimately would get the best of me. It was so bad that one day I decided to tell my teachers what was going on. Luckily, they decided not to put me in a group anymore. That was the end of my problem and it felt really good not to have to worry anymore.

One afternoon, I was late getting to the bus stop. "Wait! Wait for me!" I yelled as the driver hit the gas. I quickened my pace, hoping he'd stop if I reached the door before he accelerated. Nope, just wishful thinking.

"Darn it!" I kicked the dirt, scuffing the tip of my shoes, cursing the driver and the dirt. "I want to go home!" I moaned and groaned, watching the transport fade from sight.

I surveyed the sky. There were small grey clouds here and there, but it was mostly clear and a full rounded moon was shining up in the night sky. The moon illuminated the entire road and I opted for walking. *If I keep a steady pace, I will arrive home before midnight*, I thought. The loneliest stretch of the journey would be in the daylight and impending dusk hour. The last mile creeped me out the most, bats and all. I could run parts of the trail, shaving off time. I was prepared to take the chance. When night closed in, I'd hug the sides of the trail, blending into the brush.

Perspiration trickled down my backside and my throat ached from thirst. I reached into my sack, draining the last dribbles from my water bottle. Why hadn't I filled it before leaving school? My parents drilled into me the necessity of keeping water handy at all times. It was crucial living in the jungle. Finding oneself lost in the woods for stretches of time without water could be deadly. Dehydration killed you faster than hunger. I walked on, feeling hungry and thirsty.

One, two, three, four, five. I counted the steps to pass the time. On the hundredth step, I sprinted for approximately sixty seconds, then stopped. I walked leisurely for a spell, breathing in deeply through my nose. I switched things up and started skipping for a bit, then returned to counting my steps one by one. The time and miles passed, thanks to the stamina of a twelve-year old girl!

The man appeared out of nowhere, my tiny frame dwarfed by his heavy build. He wore muddied work boots and his shirt hung loosely outside of his pants.

"You're Segundo's daughter, aren't you?" he asked, flashing me a crooked grin. I looked at him questioningly. There was a familiarity, but something didn't sit quite right with me. I wasn't surprised he knew my father, everyone in these parts did.

"Yes, he's my father," I replied.

"Ah, I thought so. I've seen you about town with him," he said, letting his eyes sweep over my features. I felt an uncomfortable flush. My body had been changing lately and the new curves brought attention from men of all ages. "Your father helped me wrestle a small cat out of our horse pen. The cat darn near ate the horse!"

I relaxed a bit at the mention of horses.

"Really? My father wrestled a jaguar?" I said, wondering why he hadn't shared the story with me.

"No, not that big of a cat. It was an ocelot, smaller and less of a threat. They chased the cat off with rocks. Wouldn't have done that with a jag!" he said.

"So true!" I said, giggling at the thought.

We started walking and talking. The conversation led from one topic to the next and the time passed quickly. He asked me a lot of questions about school, who my friends were, and what I did when I wasn't in school. "What are you, fifteen?" he asked.

"Me, fifteen?" I said, flattered he'd think I was that old. "No, but I'm almost thirteen!" I proudly stated.

"Do you have a boyfriend?" he asked, moving in closer.

"I'm too busy for a boyfriend," I said, trying to sound mature and matter of fact. Girls were supposed to think of boys at my age, but I hadn't gotten to that point yet and my father would kill me if I brought a boy home. I didn't want to share that with him or anybody else. We walked on in silence. The conversation stopped.

I could see my brother's house in the distance; we were getting closer, but were still a bit far down the hill.

We turned the last corner and my brother's house disappeared from sight.

"It's the home stretch for me!" I said, relieved at the thought of changing my clothes and taking off my shoes. They were killing me!

"Miro," he said. "I like you." His words hung in the air waiting to be caught. I was speechless. He moved in closer, wrapping an arm around my waist. I could feel the warmth of his breath and the nasty scent of sweat. His rough hand caressed my face, neck, traveling down to my breast.

"No!" I cried, pushing him away. "I don't like you! Please leave me alone!"

He pushed me to the ground, seemingly oblivious to my cries. His hand fumbled beneath my skirt and inside my underwear. I was appalled!

"Stop! Stop!" I screamed. His fingers dove deep, tearing with each thrust of his hand. I felt the heavy weight of his body crush against me. His heart was racing and so was mine. I couldn't breathe.

"Pototo!" I screamed, hoping he could hear me from his house down the hill.

"Shut up!" the man yelled, jumping off of me. "There's nobody out here!"

Yet I continued calling my brother's name, hoping that somehow he would hear my cries. "My brother lives close by. We are very close to his house. You'd better run! If he catches you, he'll kill you!" I said, trying to get rid of him.

Then all of a sudden a shotgun blast rang through the air. "Miro, is that you? Are you okay? Answer me!" I heard my brother's voice in the distance and yelled back.

"Over here, Pototo! Hurry!" I was so thankful he was coming to my rescue.

My brother rounded the corner, shotgun in hand and a crazed look in his eyes. "What are you doing? Why are you on the ground, Miro? You're all dirty! You've been crying!" The words were stuck in my throat. I began to cry.

"He, he, hurt me! He tried to rape me!" I pointed in the direction of the running man, but he was long gone.

My brother walked me back home and he shared the story with my father. He was furious. They both were. My dad told me, "You are a foolish girl, Miro! You should know better what happens to girls that hang around boys his age! They want only one thing from girls!" The look in my father's eyes frightened me. I was crushed because my dad believed that I had put myself in that situation. It hurt me so much that my dad would think that about me. I started crying, wondering how my dad could believe I was looking for something like that. I was just a little girl.

"I didn't do anything, Papa! I was coming home from school and met him on the trail. He said he knew you. That you had helped his father chase away the cat in their horse pen!" I cried.

My father's eyes glazed over. He took my brother off to the side and they talked for a bit. My brother was listening intently to my father's words. He shook his head yes, and left.

About a week or so later, a man paid a visit to our home. It was the father of the guy that had intended to rape me.

"I am looking for my son. Have you seen him, Segundo? It's unlike him to go for so long without coming home."

My father looked from me to my brother and then at the man. "No, I haven't seen your son. I'll ask around and let you know if I hear anything," he patted the man on the back. "Do not worry. I am sure he will find his way home soon." The man left. We never spoke of him, or the man from the trail, again.

But, as little as I was, I knew what had happened to his son. It was the jungle justice, the law of the jungle: Nobody tries to hurt Segundo's daughter or his family.

# *That's Not Love*

Raul was fifteen years my senior. At fifteen, the age difference seemed a lifetime apart to the outside world, but not to my teenage mind.

"I haven't done this before, Raul," I breathlessly whispered into his ear.

He pulled back, "You haven't had sex with anyone, seriously?"

"No, never," I said, afraid he'd think I was a child.

"Do you want me to stop, Miro?" he asked, running his fingers through my hair. I looked into his eyes and then silently agreed to my first encounter.

He swept me off my feet and was my first love. Secret love, really, because nobody knew about him back at my farm. I told everyone that I had found a job in the city as a housekeeper and that allowed me enough time to attend school and do my homework so my family wouldn't get worried about my whereabouts. I knew that if my family knew of him, he'd be killed in the blink of an eye.

On my school breaks, I would let my thoughts wander to him and how good he made me feel. I wondered if the butterflies in my stomach would ever cease to flutter. Would I continue feeling nervous, giddy, scared, happy, and beautiful, indefinitely? This must be love! Now looking back at those days, I can't stop thinking that I was still just a little girl and my first love was just a pedophile taking advantage of my innocence. In a way, I was looking for a father, someone to run to when I needed to feel safe and secure. Raul seemed to have taken the place of that so sought father figure while I was in the city.

I had moved in with him and a few months later, on my way back to our place from school, something caught me by surprise. I entered the house and heard two voices coming from the back of the room. It sounded like my sister. Why was she there at my boyfriend's house?

"Hello! Is everything all right?" I yelled, knocking on the door.

"No, everything is not all right!" my sister sobbed.

"Can I come in?" I said, turning the knob. To my disbelief, Raul was in the room.

"What? What are you two doing? Raul?" I asked, looking from one to the other.

"He forced me," she whimpered.

"Right," he said, in an emotionless tone. "You wanted it," he started pulling up his pants and putting on his shirt.

All of a sudden the room started to spin. I swayed, reaching for something to hold on to. He reached out to me, the stink of alcohol on his breath.

"Get your hands off of me!" I shouted, knees buckling. "My sister, Raul? How could you? I love you! I was going to be your wife!"

He laughed. "Stop being so dramatic. She's used merchandise. It meant nothing." I couldn't believe my ears.

"Get out! Go!" he yelled at us. We left, I was too angry to talk to him, and although he tried to talk to me, I wasn't willing to listen to his excuse at the moment.

I came back a few days later because I had nowhere else to go. That was also my place, the house where I'd been living with him for the last months. And besides, I really wanted to make it work. I was so naive, I had forgiven him, I had forgiven both of them, but it hurt me very deeply to find him in bed with my sister, so much that even today, I can still feel the pain.

We tried to go on with our lives and shortly after the incident, the nausea started. My severe morning sickness continued for several months. At first, I attributed it to what happened with Raul and my sister. I didn't really know what was wrong with me. The school where I was going to was very strict and run by nuns. There was no sex education back then and no one told us anything about our bodies, about the natural changes that occur to our bodies when we start having our periods. It was so confusing, just like a lot of the other changes that come with puberty.

I had started my period earlier on and now I hadn't had it for a few months but I didn't know that meant anything was wrong. I just knew I didn't feel well.

Every day after school, Raul would wait for me and take me back to his house. One day in particular I was not feeling well at all. I had a horrible day at school because of the vomiting and nausea, but the sight of him was enough to cheer me up. I was so happy and excited to see him. He waited outside the school, tapping impatiently on the steering wheel of his Ford Pinto. I got into the car and he was acting all skittish. He took me to a restaurant where I got something to eat and he drank some beer. Immediately after eating, I vomited it all up. I told him I hadn't been feeling well for a while.

He then asked me, "When was your last period?"

"About four months ago," I replied.

"Are you kidding me?" he fumed. "You're pregnant!"

When I heard that, I said to myself, *No, it's not possible, I can't be pregnant. I'm not married, I'm still in school, I'm a little girl.* I thought my dad would kill me if he ever found out about it. I told him, "Raul, my dad will kill you." We got back into his blue car and he took out some white powder and snorted it up his nose. I had no idea what that stuff was but it made him even crazier.

"I can't believe you let yourself get pregnant!" he yelled, driving down the road at increasing speeds.

"It's not my fault. You're older than me, Raul, you should know better. I thought you wanted to marry me?

Wouldn't we eventually have had a family? Don't you want children, Raul?" I pleaded.

I watched his body fighting to remain in control. The muscles in his arms flexed as he gripped the steering wheel tighter.

"Slow down, please! You're scaring me!" He rounded the corner, two wheels in the air.

"I'm not going to marry a little girl," he said, sniffing and wiping the white residue in the crease of his fist.

He already had a daughter; of course he had never thought of marrying me. I was just a little girl; he only wanted to have fun with me.

"Not marry me? But you could have sex with me!" I yelled, seeing the white powder caked at the corner of his right nostril. He rambled a string of obscenities, enraged. Before I could even grasp what was happening, he leaned over, opened the passenger side of the car door and with one swoop, shoved me from the car without ever even touching the brake.

I rolled out, down the asphalt and landed in the middle of the street. Last thing I remembered hearing was the screeching sound of brakes. Luckily I didn't hit the curb with my face but, anyway, I passed out. Maybe it was the pregnancy, maybe the emotion, but that terrible sound of brakes was still alive in my head when I woke up surrounded by nurses and doctors, lying in a hospital bed.

"Miro, you're in the hospital. Your arm and leg are broken and your hip cracked. Do you remember what happened?"

Groggy, confused, and feeling like I'd been hit by a truck, I asked, "Where did you say I am?"

The doctor and nurse re-checked my vitals, reassuring that I was in the best of hands. "My baby, how is my baby?" I asked, closing my eyes and waiting for the answer. I could remember clearly that I was pregnant and I grabbed my stomach with fear. I could feel the pain and convinced myself to think that it was because of the cracked hip.

"We are so sorry," the doctor said. "You've lost the baby."

I was dismayed and shocked to hear the news. A bit afterward, the police entered my hospital room and asked me the name of the person who had tried to kill me. I answered and without hesitation, gave them Raul's address and information. Within a couple hours, the police had apprehended him. They brought him handcuffed to my room to confirm his identity. When he walked in and saw me lying in the hospital bed, he started weeping and asking for forgiveness. I didn't even want to look at him.

He was begging me, "Miro, please tell them that you love me, tell them how much we love each other, tell them that you were the one that pushed yourself out of the car."

I couldn't believe what I was hearing. He had killed my baby and attempted to kill me, and now was asking me to say that I'd gotten out of the car by choice. It was already too late for that. I'd told the police that it was him and asked them to take him out of my room; I didn't ever want to see him again.

He was later convicted on three counts. Attempted murder and murder of my unborn child, because he had killed my baby and intended to kill me, then also for sexual relations with a minor. He was condemned to a high security prison for 25 years and served his sentence on an island with other inmates who were also convicted of violent crimes.

My injuries healed, but the pain inside my heart remains today. He was my first love and what a horrible experience it was. He slept with my sister, took advantage of her, took my virginity away, and got me pregnant. Then, he tried to kill me and did kill my unborn child. I pray often to be forgiven for the hatred I

feel in my heart toward such a monster. If not for
myself, for the memory of the child I lost.

# *Working for an Education*

The desire for a better future and a better life, as well as the need for a sound, safe, and stable environment, had stripped me of my self-worth and nearly cost me my life. I dropped out of school and set aside my education until I could afford it again. By this time, I was attending high school and I didn't have enough money to pay for the books. I wasn't working or living with Raul, so I had to put everything aside and start looking for a job. I decided to move downtown to a very poor housing area, but one that was a cheap place to stay. I wanted to find a job, save money, and continue with my studies. I always knew deep down that without an education, I would never be able to be someone.

I still remember the first time my mom took me to the city to visit my sister Guadalupe, who was living there. I was only three or four years old and recall myself grabbing my mother's skirt while we were walking in the street. I was so scared in the city; everything was new to me, so many lights everywhere, and all those cars moving around that I had never seen before. It certainly was a jungle in itself, although not the sort of jungle I had known till then. That experience at such a young age sort of traumatized me, and I asked my mom not to take me to the city again.

Now, 12 years later, I found myself in the city again. My new place resembled a shack and cost me $3.00 per day. When I extended my stay, they raised it to $5.00 per day. A ratty bed and dresser occupied the tiny, cramped space. There was no bathroom. No running water. No kitchen to prepare a meal, and barely a ray of natural light. It was a modest pensión, as we call it in Spanish. Simply, it was four walls with a lumpy mattress to rest my weary body and a dresser to put my clothes. Minimalistic, but I was able to say something was all mine for the meager salary I earned working in the hair salon.

In that new place and environment, I met countless young females who, like me, moved from the countryside to the city in search for a better future, a better life, or new opportunities for their families. I started calling them "sisters".

They just wanted to find a job, too, but the city proved to be an extremely hard place to live. Most of them found themselves in such a difficult situation that if they weren't able to find a job and get some money, the only thing they could do was to become a prostitute.

"If you can find a spot to sleep, then stay," I said, looking from one sister to the other.

"No problem!" they chimed in, falling on the bed laughing. "I'm at the bottom!" one said, and the other, "I'm at the top!"

I shook my head. "Don't think so ladies, the uncomfortableness is not to be shared!"

My sisters bunked together whenever they traveled into the city. Their visits weren't the typical meet and greet. The electricity of the city fooled them into believing that it offered what they wanted and all the fun they were looking for. They craved the nightlife, naive to the whole idea and the risks. Derelicts, drunks, and the disorderly roamed the streets and the clubs reeked of sex, drugs, and opportunity. The girls, like countless others, absorbed their surroundings with blinders on.

Often I would call my girlfriends and ask them, "Hey, guys, where are you?" and go to meet them in whichever club they were in that day. It was on one of those trips when I got into trouble for the first time.

One day after working in the hair salon, I went out to party with them, ready to release some stress from work. "ID please, miss," the officer said, flashing the light in my face. I fumbled in my bag for the phony piece of identification, averting the man's gaze. He waited, positioning the light over my bag. "Have you been drinking?" he asked, as I continued to search.

"A little bit," I said, holding up two fingers and meaning just an inch. The officer continued to watch me, feigning no emotion, bored with the antics of another underage drinker.

"Name? Birthday?" he asked.

"Um. Guadalupe. Um…" I continued, unable to recall my sister's birthday or year for that matter. The ID said 33 years old.

"You look damn good for your age," he said, turning me around and putting on the cuffs.

"But I-!" I protested, at a loss for words.

"Don't bother," he said, taking my elbow and leading me to the car.

The hours passed and the cell grew both in population and stench. "Buzz kill," I grumbled to myself, feeling the effects of the alcohol wearing off. It was a first offense, so they mainly brought me in to sweat it out. I was told I could leave under the supervision of someone 18 years old or older and I was allowed one phone call. I made the call, got released, and vowed never to come back.

# *Cancer, a Terrible Illness*

My sixteenth year spiraled out of control. I was still working at the hair salon, but I began to realize that the party life was not going to lead me anywhere. I needed to straighten out my life if I wanted to succeed. It was around that year that I was hit with devastating news about my sister.

"Don't be silly. Nothing bad is going to happen to you," I said, believing it to be true.

"Miro, please tell me you'll be there for Katherine and the others," my sister implored.

Huffing, I said, "Just stop it, Elizabeth! Stop the nonsense! You're not going anywhere!" She continued until I promised what I hoped would never come true.

My oldest sister had been diagnosed a year earlier with cervical cancer. Two years earlier, she had delivered my niece Katherine. She didn't have the means to check her health regularly, so she didn't pay attention when she started hemorrhaging constantly, until it was too late. By the time she'd decided to see a doctor—at this time the bleeding and pain was too much—the cancer was too advanced. She was admitted at the oncological hospital where, after a year of dealing with chemotherapy treatments and morphine for the pain, she died at the young age of 33. Her death rocked the core of my family. She suffered terribly, both physically and emotionally. I was heartbroken. She was a beautiful woman, taken much too soon.

Our family was devastated, and my two-and-a-half-year old niece was left with her biological dad in the meantime, since I couldn't take care of her at that moment. I was still living in the little shack and it was not a place for a little girl to be. Plus, I had no idea of how to watch and care for a child. I was still a child myself.

"Come with me today, Miro. We are going to have some drinks and food at an Army base club," said my sister Guadalupe. Little did I know that night I was going to meet a person that will help me change my life in a good way. We arrived at the restaurant club house, sat down, and ordered some drinks. As I was sipping my orange juice—because I was still a minor by law and I couldn't legally drink alcohol—my eyes caught hold of a handsome figure against the wall watching me. It was "Mr. X". He was 42 years old and part of the Army's Special Forces.

I immediately felt a connection with him, and as I walked by his side on my way to the restroom, he grabbed my arm and pulled me next to him. He asked me my name, and within minutes, we were chatting like we'd known each other forever. I ended up completely forgetting about the restroom.

Mr. X was both kind and generous. He stood at 5'11" in boots, with a muscular build and black hair. He was a man with a big heart. We started dating right away. I remembered him telling me, "You're too young not to be in school, Miro. Finish your high school or work will never come easy for you. I am going to help you as much as I can but you have to promise me that you will get back to your studies". I appreciated his candor, kindness, and generosity. And I promised him to do it. He wasn't a rich man, but thanks to his financial help I was able to return to school.

# *In Search of the Perfect Job*

Eventually, I ran out of money and Mr. X was no longer there to help me out. I was back to square one, but I was happy that I'd at least gone back to school at night. This time, I was determined not to drop out again; I would finish high school at any cost. On the other hand, my housing situation still remained grim, as it was no place for a teenager. Most females living in that community sold themselves for money, and I was seriously considering the possibility of joining the profession. Sad, but true.

That hard choice came to me when I was confronted with three major exams in the upcoming weeks. I needed to buy the books to study for the exams and I didn't have a penny. I was totally broke.

*The money is easy and fast, Miro,* I said to myself. *Close your eyes and dream of something else.* My empty stomach and the strong desire to finish high school made the decision much easier for me.

"I have school books I need to buy. Could I do it one time and be done?" I asked the other girls with uncertainty in my voice.

"Of course! Do it twice and you can buy several books," they told me. Twice rang in my ears. I doubted the profession paid that well... or did it?

The snazzy black Lincoln drove up and an older gentleman, white haired and nicely dressed, smiled from behind the wheel. He rolled down the window and motioned for me. I looked around, making sure it was me he was directing his attention to. I straightened my shoulders, breathed in deeply, and sauntered on over.

"You want to take a ride, young lady?" he asked, eyes wandering over my body. I felt myself redden and almost turned to run.

"Yes, I want a ride," I said, slipping into the leather seat beside him and thinking *money, money, money.*

84

The hotel suite in itself was a treat for my eyes. If I remembered anything, it would be this room. The Jacuzzi, den, and earthy greens and browns were a perfect combination. It was warm, inviting, and comfortable. I took it all in, doubtful I'd ever set foot into a place like this again. He walked into the bathroom and closed the door.

He was probably expecting to come out of the bathroom and find me naked in the room, but I was so confused that I paced, not knowing where to begin. I decided not to take my clothes off. I was so scared of finding myself in such a situation.

*You're crazy. This is crazy. Maybe he's crazy,* I said to myself, sitting down on the edge of the bed and playing with my fingers, thinking that this wasn't going to work. I had never been before with anyone in a situation like this. Sure, I'd had sex before, but I'd never found myself offering sex for money with no feelings involved.

I lay back, closed my eyes, and tried to control the spasms rippling through my body. *Dream, Miro, and the money will be yours.*

"Are you okay?" he said, sitting down on the bed beside me. He was shirtless—I looked up at his naked chest and felt paralyzed. His chest was matted with wiry white hair. His arms were spindly and lacked muscle. His extended belly looked pregnant. I turned away, hiding my distaste. "Have you ever done this before?" he asked, concern in his voice.

"No, not for money. I need to buy school books and my job salary isn't enough," I said.

He cleared his throat and said, "College is expensive."

I continued and turned, focusing my attention on his eyes. "I hope to one day go, after I finish high school."

"You're still in high school? How old are you? Where are your parents? Your family?" He stammered and rose from the bed.

He put his shirt back on quickly, watching me closely and waiting for an answer.

"Long story," I said. "Another time, maybe."

He reached into his back pocket and pulled out a wad of bills out of his wallet, peeling off several. "Take some money, you said you need money for your books, how much do your books cost?" he said.

"I only need to buy three books sir, and it is a $146 for the three of them." I answered. He gave me a handful of bills, about $200, and I could only say, "I can't take this money sir, I haven't done anything with you."

"Please, stop calling me sir. Take this money. It's for your books, but you have to promise me that you will never put yourself in this situation again," he said. Then he looked at me and said in a serious tone, "This life is not for you, I can see in your eyes that you are determined to finish your studies. Trust me, that's what is going to give you the money you want in life. You don't need to do this." He then walked out the door and waited to take me home.

I lay in the bed for a moment, looking at the ceiling, feeling embarrassed and humiliated. Embarrassed for my reaction to the kind, generous gentleman, and humiliated for intending to sell my body.

Our conversation centered on my studies during the ride home. He asked a lot of questions about where I was in my education and where I hoped to go. He didn't ask again about my parents or any family. I was touched by his curiosity and genuine concern. I remember thinking that there were really good people in this world and that I had been really lucky to meet one of them.

When the car arrived at my door, he asked me, "Is this the place where you live? Girl, this is not a place to live."

He look surprised at the sight of the place and told me that he was going to hook me up with a friend of his, the owner of a hotel, and that he was going to ask him to hire me. "What are you working on in school? What are you going to be?" he asked, and I answered impatiently, "Accounting, I'm getting my diploma in accounting, and I'm very good at that, sir."

And so it happened that in just a few hours, I was offered an actual job in a field of my interest, accounting, as an accounting assistant to a colleague of his. My first day would be tomorrow, and a car would be sent to pick me up. I closed my eyes, afraid to dream that this was real. It was truly a miracle that I had met an angel who'd helped me to get to the next phase of my life, and I didn't have to sell my body to get there. I wanted to remember every single part of that day.

# *Plastic Boys*

I worked at the hotel as an accounting assistant and was able to finish my high school by going to night classes. I worked a normal 8-5 shift, and then went to school from 7-11pm. It was exhausting, but well worth it to get my diploma.

I was able to rent a room in a condo with an elderly lady with the money I was earning at my job. I was also able to enroll myself into college and start classes. Finishing high school with honors made me realize that I wanted to continue my education. I had a golden opportunity that most people in my country don't get.

My new house was far from the college campus, so I had to take the bus every night. The only problem was that the bus stop was located in "The Red Light District".

Once inside the parameters of "The Red Light District", there was no turning back. It was a section of town that was like sin city. There were bars on every corner and in-between. Certain areas were littered with prostitutes and wealth of varying degrees. Fancy buildings and shiny bright lights attracted the party people. I briskly walked, head down, determined not to draw attention to myself.

Every night I had to walk alone, and a girl alone at this time of the night was an easy target.

The walk to the bus was under a half mile from the college and reachable only through this particular area of the city. It wasn't a long walk, and it wasn't the first time that I was walking that path, either. Tonight, I hoped to get home earlier than usual, which would give me time to continue studying before turning in. My books were not heavy and it was an easy, peaceful walk for me. Stopping to rest wasn't necessary, so I trudged forward, seeking the relief that lay ahead.

I heard a low whistle as a vehicle approached from behind. "Can I offer you a ride, pretty lady?" he asked, feigning innocence and charm. I stepped up my pace, determined not to look in the direction of the voice. I could hear the tires crunch the ground as the Jeep continued its path along my left side. I couldn't outrun it, so I turned, preparing to ward off his advances in the most polite manner possible.

"Thank you, but I'm catching the bus up around the corner," I said, knowing the proximity was a bit farther.

"Boo hoo! You're no fun!" he jokingly said, flashing the most beautiful set of pearly whites.

The banter carried on beyond the corner and imaginary pickup point. To my surprise, I found myself giddy and enjoying the easy conversation. I noticed his wheels were as nice as his smile. Maybe he was a good guy after all.

The Jeep had dark windows, so I could only see the driver. However, he was really cute. "Come on, I'll give you a ride." And I thought, *What the heck, he's really cute, has a nice car, and clearly does have money. Who knows? Maybe we'll start dating.*

I opened the car door, and immediately I felt something in my gut twisting, my sixth sense was in full alert. I felt a sort of premonition and could feel a voice telling me not to do it, telling me that something bad was going to happen to me. Unfortunately, it was too late to back up. I got in the seat. And as soon as I sat down, the windows went up and locks went down. I went cold. I felt a darkness overcome me and the muscles in my back and neck tighten. My heart pounded in my chest, and the hair on the back of my neck stood on end. Thoughts of escape raced through my mind.

"Don't make a sound or scream or you're dead." I felt the steel of a gun against my head and heard a voice from the back of my seat. The muscles in my back and neck tightened. I held up my hands and nervously said, "Please don't shoot me!"

He said, "Didn't I tell you not to make a sound?" and pressed the gun even harder against my neck. I shut up and started crying. I knew I was in big trouble.

For the first few minutes, I could not tell how many people were in the car since I couldn't move or make any noise. But after an agonizing silence and 10 minutes or so of driving, I started listening to their voices and recognized that there were at least three of them, the driver and two in the back seat. The two in the back had been crouched on the floor, listening and waiting for the foolish girl to be lured into the vehicle.

"Where are we going?" I asked, knowing the answer wouldn't be to my liking. The good-looking driver said nothing. He concentrated on the road, neither looking at me or the two in the back. I started to nervously chatter. "The bus picks me up back there. I can still make it if you drop me now. There might be another-" I was stopped in mid-sentence.

"I told you to shut up," he said.

They drove on for 40 minutes more, leaving the lights of the city and the areas of Panama that were familiar to me behind. The sight of trees and dense forest offered little comfort. I felt the panic rising.

After what seemed like an eternity, we finally arrived at a big three-story mansion. They got me from the car with a gun at my back. I fell on my knees.

"Please let me go!" I begged. "I'll say nothing to anyone. I didn't hear anything or see anything. I won't do anything!" I tried to convince myself there was still a way out. Laughter drowned out my pleas and I was at the mercy of three ruthless men.

I was basically dragged from where the Jeep had parked to the main entrance. I was resistant to go inside the house because I knew it will be a miracle to come out alive since I had already seen their faces and had a horrible feeling. I could sense they were cruel and merciless men. They shoved and pushed me into the house and when one of them opened the front door, I was overcome with despair worried that I might never see the sunlight or my family again. It was pitch black but since I grew up in the jungle without any electricity, or technology, all my senses had developed very well and I was able to see better than them.

I noticed two halls and few closed doors along both halls. I then was pushed to the left side where one of them opened a door to a room that was dimly lit, windowless, and smelled of stale air and a nasty scent of sweat. A glass table occupied its center, covered with small mounds of white powder, a blade for cutting, and bills rolled out like little tubes. The color reminded me of what Raul used to put up his nose. I scanned the outskirts of the room, noticing a small worn couch and two folding chairs. On the floor beside the couch, rested a large suitcase filled with $100 bills. The contents spilled over the sides, causing the crisp greens to spread out and under the couch.

"What are you looking at?" the driver spat, before pushing me through the space with a force that knocked me to my knees.

"I wasn't looking at anything!" I said, trying to rise, only to be pushed to my knees again. The same man grabbed my hair and placed a pistol to my face, caressing it with the cold tip.

"Please no," I whimpered, afraid he'd strike me with the butt of the gun.

"Get naked!" he said, turning to the table and forming a long, thin line of white powder, then snorting it up his nose in one quick sniff.

I didn't want to take my clothes off because I knew what was going to happen next. Then, one of the guys kicked me in the ribs and I started crying. It hurt so bad, it was a pain I can't even describe. All I could think of was my mother. I wanted my mother so badly, for her to come and rescue me and to be in her safe arms.

Two of the men came over and ripped my clothes off me as I was lying on the floor. They stripped me down until I was completely naked. The driver came over first; he was the biggest of the three men. He forced himself onto me. Tears rolled down my face. The only thing keeping me alive was my thoughts of my mother and horse. My body lay lifeless in this house of horrors, but my mind was back in the jungle, racing my beautiful horse. I could feel his soft mane against my cheek and smell the fresh air. For just a moment, my soul lifted from my body, like I wasn't even there. Instead, it was like a movie I was watching from outside myself. For just a second, I was back in the farm... It almost seemed peaceful...

SMACK! One of the men hit me hard in the face and brought me back to the severity of reality. Blood gushed down my face. I was so bloody, I could barely see. He pulled my hair up and I looked down, watching all that blood coming out of my face. At that moment, I knew that those three beasts were going to kill me, that I wouldn't be able to escape from there alive.

The three of them took turns raping and beating me. They used the white powder to numb their senses and also sprinkled it on my breasts, between my legs, and anywhere else they wanted to lick, tearing at flesh in the process. My lips and gums were bloodied and numb. I no longer felt the power of their bites or the pull, as they devoured pieces of me, leaving my skin marked and bruised.

"Stop! Please stop!" I begged them, fighting a fight to save my life. My resistance and screams did little to deter the onslaught of male dominance, insanely intent on breaking my spirit and taking my life. I was punched, kicked, and entered with a force that tore each and every opening, leaving a trail of blood on whatever it touched. My cries increased the frequency of attack, leaving my battered body beaten and defenseless on the cold cement floor.

I wanted to die. Please just shoot me.

For a moment, I contemplated that possibility, but there was something inside me that made me believe there was a way out, that something would eventually happen and I would have a chance to get away.

The pain from the beatings and constant rape was so immense, I couldn't take it anymore. I was no longer a woman, but a piece of meat used and tossed aside. I was so torn apart after so many blows to my body, I had stopped feeling, and felt dead.

"Let's leave this bitch here and get the other ones!" one of the men roared, signaling for the tall man to join him. "You, stay here!" he commanded to the shorter, chubby one. "Watch her carefully!" he said, walking across the room, toward the screams coming from the other end of the house. Through my delirium, I watched their two backs float out the door.

"Mama," I whispered, my face swollen against the chill of the hard floor. "I should've listened to your words, warning me never to get into a stranger's car. I am so sorry, Mama. I love you." I drifted off, hearing screams in the distance, too tired to comprehend. I felt comforted by the vision of my mother's warm embrace and the thought of my horse running wild and free.

"Wake up!" the smaller man blurted, nudging me hard in the side of my ribs with the toe of his dress shoes. My body lay in his arms, listless. He straddled me from behind; however, he could no longer keep an erection from either too much drinking or the powder. Frustrated, he retreated to the couch.

That was my saving grace.

I watched him doze off, oblivious to the fact that I was now awake and thinking of a way out.

I crawled naked to the door with every last ounce of energy I had left in me, peeking around the corner into the hall. I didn't stop to grab my clothes; now that the other guys were not in the room, all I had in my mind was how to get out of there.

Everything was clear. Even though I had blood in my eyes, I could see perfectly. When they first brought me in, I had made a mental note of everything and now that clear picture of this place was helping me find a way out of that horrible house. I made my way down the narrow stretch to the door at the opposite end. My heart raced at the anticipation of freedom.

Behind me, a loud gunshot went off in the house, followed by the highest pitched scream I've ever heard in my life. Her cries pierced my body, and I knew she was suffering horribly.

I looked over my shoulder and nervously considered the option of going back. I knew that these women were suffering the same abuses as me. I thought, *Should I go back and try to help the others, or should I save myself?* I didn't even know how many people were there. I thought of the other women that undoubtedly would leave this earth, having been raped, tortured, and most likely shot. I felt bad for leaving them behind, but if I did not get out now, I would be dead, too.

I grabbed the knob, gently easing it back, trying to soften the whine. As I pulled open the door, fresh jungle air breezed across my face. I breathed it in, deeply filling my lungs. I could then see the leaves off in the distance. It never looked more beautiful. I knew if I could just make it there, I would survive.

The big elaborate entrance to the mansion lay just ahead. My body was so weak and tired. I was completely naked and covered in blood. I don't know where the strength came from, but I dragged my beaten body to the jungle's edge and rose to my feet. Once I got myself past the parking spot and into the jungle, I heard the door from the mansion swing open. The other men were in the doorway screaming to the fat one, "How could you let her get away!"

I panicked, thinking they would catch up to me. So I jumped like a panther into the brush, leaping through the air in one graceful bound and landing on the other side, feeling the cold dirt between my toes. I let out a huge breath once nestled within the foliage. I turned and could see them in the dim lights of the porch, but they could not see me. I was now in my territory. The Little Amazonian had regained her jungle senses, and no one, not anyone, was going to hurt her again!

I ran far into the jungle, which seemed to be a couple miles. I ran so far and so fast I barely noticed my feet bloody from the thorns and bushes. Finally, I made it out of the jungle to a road. I could see old houses and more street lights; what I didn't know in that moment is that I was in one of the most dangerous areas of the city. Drugs users and dealers were everywhere. I collapsed in the middle of the road and saw the yellow lights of a cab. Upon sighting me, it screeched to a stop and an old man jumped out.

"Dear God, child, what has happened to you?" he stammered, not believing his eyes. He removed his shirt and gently wrapped it around my naked, bloody, trembling body.

"Please help me," I said, drifting into unconsciousness.

I woke in the hospital to questions I couldn't answer. "No. I don't know. No," I said. The hospital, its staff, and the police all took turns, searching for answers I didn't have. "I took a ride from a cute guy in The Red Light District, while walking to the bus from college. I was taken to an unknown location. No, I didn't know where I was and they drugged me and repeatedly raped me. I escaped after the guy who was guarding me fell asleep on the couch. I ran for two miles or more to get far away. Well, I could barely walk, but it felt like running to me, I was barefoot, naked, and completely covered in blood, but I survived."

Their faces said it all. Girl out looking for a good time in a bad area gets what she deserves. I shook my head, crying and repeating, "I told you no. I don't know by who or why or where I was taken or the location of any drugs or money." I was medically treated and released, then dressed in what looked like discarded rags.

I decided to rent a room at the place where I lived before. I stayed there for a week because there was no way I could tell the elderly lady at the condo what had happened to me. I needed time for my broken bones, swollen face, and other parts of my body to heal. Painkillers and antibiotics were prescribed to me. Nobody paid any attention to me or my broken body in the old place. I dealt with the physical and emotional pain all alone.

About a week or so later, five female bodies were discovered in a landfill site. The women had been stripped of their clothing and burned beyond recognition. I remembered thinking about what I'd heard one of them say to the others "After we're done with these bitches, we're going to burn their bodies. There won't be anything left, so nobody can recognize them and there'll be no trails back to us." I knew at that moment that I'd escaped death and that I was a survivor. The case remained open, but it went cold. It was assumed that the women were prostitutes and were therefore unworthy of society or justice.

It made my blood boil to think that these men could do whatever they wanted to a woman and not pay for their crimes. I assumed that they were rich and packed with money due to the big house and the large amount of drugs and cash on the table. People like that were called Plásticos, because nothing can stick to them or hurt them. Their families were also wealthy and prosperous and had enough money to get them out of any crimes they'd committed. Sadly, in most of our third world countries, the rich and privileged can get away with everything with no punishment at all.

# *Wedding Bells & Baby Blues*

After the life-altering incident with the "Plásticos", I settled back into my life the best I could. I returned to the accounting assistant job, while continuing to look over my shoulder during the day and wrestle with the demons at night, vowing not to surrender to any ghosts of my past. Easier said than done, but religiously practiced from one day to the next.

I met the man I would marry in the most ordinary way. "Ordinary" being my new mantra. He came into my place of employment, and that was that. The deal was sealed. It wasn't love at first sight and I wasn't smitten, but there was something there and I wanted it. Although he didn't carry a weapon, his quiet demeanor calmed me and his position as an Air Force Duty Sergeant made me feel comfortable. After last year's events I'd come to the realization that military men in general made me feel safe. It also could be the fact that military men are conditioned to serve, protect, and honor people and the country we live in.

The suggestion that we get engaged came after a visit from my boyfriend's captain. "Is it a serious relationship between you and that girl?" he asked, waiting for an answer. My boyfriend was taken aback by his superior's interest. "If you're not serious, I'd like to ask her out."

Later that same day, we got engaged. When I saw his captain, I gave a big hello and secretly thanked him for the push.

Little by little, I left my belongings at Mark's condo. "Why not bring it all here?" he asked, as if it was a natural choice to make. He didn't have to ask twice. I cleared out my place, moved in with him, and a year and a half passed in the blink of an eye.

The move, the engagement, and the upcoming nuptials had me thinking long and hard about the sister

I'd lost to cancer and the promise I'd made to her to take care of her youngest child. Supposedly, my brother-in-law battled with the bottle, played the field, toured with his band, and often left my niece in the hands of a variety of friends and acquaintances. My mother was distraught with worry. "The child is developing psychological issues, Miro, and there's nothing we can do about it!"

Unfortunately, I had been trying to raise myself for a while and didn't feel suitable as a parent. Furthermore, I couldn't afford to care for all of my sister's three children. The oldest was a girl of 13, a boy who was 11, and the youngest was two. The little money I was making was barely supporting me.

With the engagement and wedding coming up, I felt more confident about fulfilling my promise to my sister. I started having my niece, Katherine come over and stay with me and Mark.

"Your mother loves you to the moon and back," I said, tucking her in one night.

"Mommy's up there?" she asked, pointing to the sky.

"Yes, Mommy is there and she is also here," I said, placing my hand on the child's heart. Her small hand covered mine, her eyes closed, and she drifted off to sleep in an instant. I watched her for moment or two.

The hair, nose, and eyes hidden under the long lashes all reminded me of my sister. "She is safe, sissy." I whispered, walking from the room and wiping the tears.

Mark and I set our wedding date for July 4th, after a two-year engagement. We did both a speedy courthouse ceremony and a more intimate church ceremony, which enabled us to share the day with family and friends. Neither was lavish. I held a single white orchid at the courthouse, and at my mother's insistence, the wedding flowers consisted of white orchids and a variety of colorful flowers.

Once I was married and moving on with my life as a functional adult, my mind kept tugging at me of the promise I made to my sister. I wanted to be able to keep that promise to her.

"Let's adopt Katherine," I said, hoping Mark would like the idea.

"Adopt, Miro? Why would we do that?" he asked. "One day we'll have children of our own. I worry that the kid is messed up. She's five and your sister was gone when she was two. I doubt I could commit to that, especially knowing she's not really mine."

I shook my head and paced the kitchen. "That's exactly the problem, Mark. She doesn't really belong to anyone. My sister is gone, her dad is absent most of the time, and the poor girl is passed amongst God knows who on a daily basis."

He didn't respond, but sat looking perplexed, and I got my way!

Katherine came to live with us and we did our best to raise her as our own. I exercised more of a dual role, being both mother and father to her. Mark's approach to parenting was carefree, whereas mine centered on structure and empowerment. I wanted rules, but I also wanted Katherine to grow up speaking her mind and seeking a place in the world. I encouraged her to be ambitious in her studies and nurtured her creative side, too. Craft night was the best!

Discipline was another area where Mark and I divided the line. Even though he was military, he grew up under one roof as the youngest child of four and was sort of "mommy's little boy". A scolding from him wasn't serious, considering he is both giving and kind. I, on the other hand, had little given to me. Discipline came at the hand of both parents, usually in the form of tree branches or switches, which were like the whips used on livestock, cows and horses. Katherine got some of both worlds. Her stepfather used pacification techniques. I used both corporal punishment and hugs.

I had the good fortune of being able to return to school and continue my studies. I excelled in ESL classes, but bombed history. I suppose I wanted to learn more English than dates in time. The school path diverted when I got pregnant and lost the baby at four months. "It's my fault!" I cried, blaming myself for the loss. I blamed the doctors, God, and anyone else that was connected to me. I spiraled downward, depression consuming me. I had a case of the baby blues and I had it bad. The psychological trauma took its toll. At one point the chaplain paid a visit to my home. His words were lost on me. He'd leave, and I'd blame him, too.

The depression worsened and my headaches returned. I developed a dependency on Tylenol. I took one a day, most days. My normal disposition went from cheery to sour grapes. I became downright mean and eventually worried that Katherine would fear me. Losing an unborn child was devastating enough, I didn't want to lose the little girl I'd made my own. She'd had enough loss in her own life. I was supposed to be her rock, not the weight that drowned her. The day she asked, "Why are you so sad?" was the day I knew I needed to change. I busied my mind and hands by enrolling in pottery classes, painting, and crochet. My focus returned to college and I spread my wings by expanding my group of friends, too. Nine months later, I was blessed with another pregnancy.

The hormones took center stage, and the pregnancy became a burden. My husband shared the news that he was required by the military to do one more overseas assignment, and that we'd have to move to whatever location they had available for him. To top things off, my doctor phoned, advising me that additional blood tests were needed to check my condition.

"You've tested positive for toxoplasmosis, Miro, and it can damage the baby if at a high percentage," he said, concern rising in his voice.

"You're kidding me, right?" I said, not even asking for the definition of such a condition.

"You get it by coming in contact with cat feces. It is only a worry for pregnant women."

My jaw dropped. "That's ridiculous!" I said, clearly in denial.

"You have to be checked. If 100% conclusive, then I'd recommend aborting the child. If not, you'd be facing raising a child that suffers from retardation." My world stopped.

I went ahead with the testing, just to be sure. I still remember the exact words the doctor said when we met with him for the results. "The test came back positive for the virus, but it isn't active and poses no risk to the fetus, Miro," he said, reassuring me the pregnancy was going to be fine and that I'd deliver a healthy baby. Relief swept over me. My husband and I took a drive, enjoying the happy news, and making plans for the arrival of our child. Life felt back on track.

On the way back from the doctor, we drove by a house I remembered. It was strange at first, knowing you have been someplace before but can't put your finger on it. Then all of a sudden, a chill took over my body. My eyes grew big and memories flashed back of the amount of physical and mental pain that had been inflicted on me in that house before.

"That's it! That's the house!" I said, blurting the words into my husband's ear as he drove slowly by.

"Oh, you lived there as a child?" he asked, looking over the property with interest.

"No! Not the house I grew up in! It's the house where I almost lost my life!" I said.

He looked confused. "What?"

I looked at his eyes and realized that I couldn't share that horrible experience with him. I was still ashamed and felt guilty for what had happened to me that day, so I lied to him and made up a silly story. He believed me, and we didn't talk more about it.

The news of moving to Japan happened when I was seven months pregnant. My biggest worries were the language barrier, the pregnancy, and the fact that I had never been away from my family. We were traveling to a country that spoke Japanese, not Spanish or English. The surroundings alone were enough to take in. No, it didn't feel like a vacation. It was pretty hectic and depression started getting to me, mostly because I was missing my family terribly.

I was alone and pregnant, taking care of Katherine. Mark was always off working and I felt that I had no support. We were living in a temporary lodging facility for three months. All day long, I was stuck in the room because I didn't know how to drive and I didn't speak the native tongue or enough English to make any friends.

The depression finally took over and I dropped into a state of despair. I was engulfed with dark feelings. My hormones at the time only made my helplessness worse. I wanted to kill myself and end my desperation once and for all. So, I took an entire bottle of pills. I fell into a deep sleep and dreamt of a fatherly figure whom I came to the conclusion was God. The man in my dream was upset. He was angry at me for wanting to kill myself and my unborn baby. Before he left my dream, he whispered to me, "It's going to be a boy and you will name him Christopher, you will be fine, and you don't have to worry about anything anymore."

I woke groggy and confused, but managed to get myself out bed, get dressed, and get to church on time.

I never told Mark that I wanted to hurt myself though. Later on that day when we returned home, I started to feel nauseated. "Are you okay, Miro?" Mark asked, taking my arm and leading me to the chair. "You look pale. Let me get you a glass of water."

Before I realized it, we were heading to the hospital. "Is it time?" my husband said, turning to look at the nurse.

"It's not time!" I cried, as the nurse inserted the needle into my cervix. "He needs more time to grow!" I sobbed, unable to stop the tears. The pills that I had taken the night before, along with my depression and stress, had made me start having contractions when I was only 32 weeks into my pregnancy. Thank God, the shot they gave me stopped the contractions and closed my cervix. I was sent back home for another nine weeks.

Then, at 41 weeks into my pregnancy, the contractions started again. But this time I was ready for it. Mark drove me to the hospital and I was told that I was ready to deliver my baby. The nurse and doctor reassured us that it was the right time. Christopher Brian Taylor was born around 3am on a Sunday, weighing 9 healthy pounds and 6 ounces, as ready for this world as he could be.

# *Brain Tumor*

Since my son Christopher's birth, I had been continuously in pain and having terrible headaches almost every day. I was taking so much Tylenol to stop the headaches, but nothing seemed to work. My eyesight was continuously becoming blurred and finally a doctor in downtown Japan prescribed me reading glasses, thinking that it was the reason for my headaches.

At that time, I didn't want to leave my son with anyone and decided to become a family day care provider to get the problem solved. I established my business in the house and used one of the rooms as my classroom. I was working very hard, waking up at 3am and taking care of children throughout the whole day. And I was attending college in order to complete my Associates. Life was good! I liked the idea of having Christopher with me while I was caring for the other children, and I was also earning good money. Additionally, I was studying in order to prepare for my interview to become an American citizen.

However, since we were stationed at an American base in Japan, I needed to get to Hawaii in order to complete my citizenship. So, we decided to go on vacation to Hawaii and kill two birds with one stone. We had to travel from Japan to Osaka and from there, to Hawaii, but when we landed in Osaka, my headaches were completely unbearable. I was very dizzy and going through a lot of pain. It felt like someone was putting a needle in the back of my head and I completely blacked out. When I woke up a month later, I received the tragic news of having a benign tumor in my hypothalamus.

I had been flown from Osaka to Hawaii and stayed in the hospital for over a month. I had been in coma this whole time. I had no idea where this tumor came from. Then all of a sudden I recalled my fall from the cashew tree when I was a little girl. I'd never gone back to the doctor to see if that blood clot had dissipated, and this tumor was in the same location that the blood clot had been. I then realized it had not gone away and instead became something more. They did surgery while I was in the coma and removed half of the tumor. The doctors could not remove all of it because I would have lost most of my long-term memory. The coma was medically-induced because I'd previously been taking so much Tylenol that my liver enzymes were really high. As my liver was seriously damaged, they needed to stabilize both the tumor and the liver.

This was another close call with death. I'm happy I survived, but unfortunately, I missed the appointment for my citizenship interview.

After I got released from the hospital, my husband informed me that he was able to reschedule my interview so now I was able to attend after all. I was very happy because I wanted it so much. I was released on a Monday and that following Friday I had my appointment.

The lady who interviewed me was very nice. "Who was the first President of the United States?" she asked me. Even though my head was a mess, I knew the answer to that question. Then she told me, "Get a piece of paper, get a pen, and write down 'I want to be a United States citizen'. I did it.

"Did you go to college?" she asked.

"Yes, I got my Associate's Degree and I'm working toward my Bachelor's," I said.

"And do you work?" she asked next.

"Yes, I work," I answered.

I had to know how to speak and write English properly to be able to get my citizenship. And I passed! I was so excited.

The next Monday, I was sworn in at the ceremony and received my citizenship certificate. Despite the happiness, anyone could tell by my face that I was sick.

We traveled back to Japan. The doctors decided not to do any further surgeries at that time and to treat the remains of the tumor with medication, hoping to shrink it.

Two years went by without any further incidents; neurologists were monitoring my brain mass in order to see if there were any changes to it. Every six months, I had a CAT scan. I was getting treated with medications and chemotherapy in order to reduce the size.

Then, my husband got orders to retire in Mississippi. We arrived in Biloxi in 2004. I started going to the gym, working out, and losing weight. I was getting leaner by the day and feeling great!

Six weeks after our arrival, our remaining belongings were delivered to us in boxes. It was like Christmas morning! I ripped through them to see what was inside. I couldn't remember half of what we packed. Then I opened the box that contained my wedding dress. I was a little bit chunky when I got married, so I wanted to see how much better I looked in it now.

I took the dress out of the box and slipped into it with ease. It was so big! It hung off my shoulders like a huge sack. I was so excited! I put the high heels on and my veil and thought, *I want to show my husband how much weight I've lost.* I started walking quickly down the hallway to his office within the house, but suddenly I felt like someone smacked me in the back of my head with a hammer. That is the last thing I remember.

Three months later, I woke up from a coma with amnesia. I couldn't remember who I was or even that I had a son. I was informed that several times they had to put me into an induced coma because of the pain, but I couldn't remember anything. Off to my right, there stood a priest and a man holding a child. I didn´t know who they were. I had no recollection of anything. I had no idea where I was or who I was.

I looked up at the child the man was holding, and I started crying for no reason. There was certainly a connection that made me feel that way even if I wasn't aware of who they were, that man with the child. Suddenly, the child was moving toward me; he wanted to be with me. "Mommy, Mommy," he said.

"But who am I? Where am I? What happened?" I was so desperate that I started to grab my head trying to remember what had happened to me. Eventually they showed some pictures of my induced coma state, but I still couldn't believe it. I couldn't believe that I had been gone for so long. There was nothing in my head. No nightmares, no dreams, nothing.

Doctors said my tumor had grown bigger and caused a vein in my brain to rupture. Miraculously, the doctors were able to clip the damaged vein and removed more of the tumor. They didn't remove all of it. They left a part of the tumor that was embedded in the long term memory, the thalamus. If they took all of it, my entire long-term memory would be gone forever.

It was a week later when I actually remembered the name of my son, Christopher. When my son heard me calling him by his name, he was the happiest child in the world. I could hold him and touch him, knowing that he was my son. Later on, I remembered my mom and my daughter Katherine, but not my husband yet. A few days after that, I was finally able to remember him as well. I started to slowly regain memories. It took me awhile to finally remember most things.

My husband told me that when he found me in the hallway of our home, my veil and part of the dress was completely covered in blood. He said I had blood coming from my eyes, my nose, my mouth, and my ears, everywhere. Everyone thought I was going to die. They brought a priest to give me the last rituals. It was at that moment that I awoke. It was truly a miracle that I survived.

To this day, I still have memory lapses from my childhood. I can't remember everything about my high school and middle school. There are some faces and names I don't recall, either. Everything seems to be buried somewhere inside my head. Like in a dream.

"Do you remember your uncle, Miro? Do you remember Jorge? My brother, Miro. He died," said my mom one day when she came over to visit me.

"Mom, I'm sorry, I can't," I said. That saddens me a lot. I was very close to him and would often go to his farm to steal his oranges. But all of that is completely gone now.

# *Divorce*

In 2006, my adopted goddaughter Katherine was in her early teens and my son was a young boy. I still wanted to have a daughter of my own, but my marriage was going badly. We would argue all the time. He wasn't doing anything to help with the children or the house. I was being supermom, doing everything myself. I knew that my marriage wasn't going to survive. I figured I might as well be by myself since I'm doing everything on my own anyway. So, I filed for divorce and we separated, but we were still living in the same house. It was during that time that I was experiencing more headaches and I started bleeding from my nose. Whenever I sneezed, there was blood.

All this time I had been seeing a neurologist. I was getting CAT scans every six months to monitor my tumor, but it was still there with no changes. A week after I filed for divorce, I received a phone call.

"Mrs. Taylor," the doctor said. "We got your CAT scan results. What are you doing?"

I said, "I'm driving."

She asked me to pull over, so right then I knew something was wrong. She asked if anyone was with me, and I said no, but that she could tell me what it was anyway.

*Don't let it be another brain tumor*, I prayed to God. *Don't let that happen.*

"We reviewed your CAT scans and you have a growth," she said.

"What?" I asked.

"You have a huge mass on your frontal sinus cavities," the doctor said again.

They told me it was on my frontal lobes in the brain and was covering 50% of my sinus cavity, putting pressure on my brain, which is what was causing the bleeding and the pain. Then they told me I needed to see an ENT surgeon immediately because it was growing fast.

I went home and Mark was there. I let him know the bad news. At this time I wasn't working, so I was dependent upon his medical insurance. Right after you file for divorce is not the best time for more health issues.

He said, "If you want to keep my insurance, I'll make you a deal. I want primary custody of my son." Since Christopher was his biological child, he wanted primary custody and for me to pay child support.

I told Mark I couldn't, that I didn't have any money, but he had no sympathy left for me at that time, and told me I had no choice.

I felt like the whole world just wanted to swallow me. I was in pain. The world was causing so much pain.

What else? What was I doing wrong, God? Is this some kind of punishment? But it's not. It wasn't like that. It's not God's fault. I guess bad things just happen to me. I ended up accepting Mark's terms. I knew that if I died, Mark would be granted custody anyway. I had no other way to pay the medical expenses without the insurance. So, I agreed to his terms and then contacted the ENT surgeon. A month prior to the scheduled surgery, I got a job with the state, but I still couldn't use that insurance.

Surgery was performed and I was in the hospital all alone. My co-worker drove me to and from the surgery. Thank goodness it was only an outpatient procedure taking 4-5 hours, including recovery time. The cause ended up being bacteria I caught while living back in Panama. It developed into polyps in the front of my brain and created a huge mass that caused a lot of pain. They were able to successfully remove all of the mass.

After the surgery, I moved out of the house. Katherine at this point didn't seem to care about me or anyone else. She was growing up and always getting in trouble. She wanted to have sex at 14. She wanted a cell phone. She wanted a car. She wanted everything. She was at the age of assuming she knew more than I did. She told me she wanted to stay with her dad. Mark does love her, even though he is her adopted father, so, I couldn't fight that. I mean, she was 14. She knows.

"You're a mean mom" she told me. "You're a witch. You spank me all the time. You yell at me, you don't understand me. You treat me differently than your son. It's not my fault that my mom died. You should have never adopted me. You should have left me with my real father."

"You know, Katherine," I said. "One day you'll become a mom and maybe one day you will understand what I am trying to do for you. I want the best for you. I don't want you to do drugs, I don't want you to smoke weed. I don't want you to have sex at 14 years old. That's not right. I am doing this for you just because I want you to be a better person. I am not doing this because I want to be mean."

I ended up having to pay child support for my son and for Katherine. She decided that she wanted to stay with her dad after we divorced and never wanted to see me again. I only get to see Christopher every other weekend. He was young then, but now he understands what I went through for him. We have a very close bond. We talk about anything. He can ask me about anything: sex, drugs, anything. He's a very smart child.

# *Monica*

Mark and I were officially divorced in 2008. I moved on with my life and was settling in with my new job.

I was moving forward and set out to achieve some lifetime goals. It took me two years and I did it online, but I finally acquired my Master's Degree in Science for Human Resource Management. With my higher education, I received a raise from my employer.

Around this time, I met someone and I got married for a second time in 2009 to a former Delta Operator. We have a beautiful daughter together, Monica. I really wanted a biological daughter of my own. It just wasn't the same with my niece. It's not Katherine's fault at all, as I know the fault lies with me; but I was barely a child myself when I adopted her.

I always knew I was going to have my own little girl to nurture. I knew it was in the cards for me. And when it finally happened, it was the right moment in my life for her to come.

However, my pregnancy with Monica was not an easy one. It was a really tough 9 months. Most of the time I was on my own as my husband was traveling to make a living. He was often away and was not the nurturing type of guy I thought he was going to be. I pretty much went through the pregnancy by myself.

I even remember one time, when I was eight weeks along, we were moving and he asked me to move some heavy furniture in our house. He didn't seem to care that I was holding a child in my belly. The effort was so tremendous that I started spotting and had to rush to the hospital. I thought I had lost her, but luckily my miracle baby was still there. I was so thankful and utterly happy. However, the father didn't seem to feel the same way. I don't think he really wanted to have children with me. I felt he just wanted someone to have fun with. Not a family.

So, I started attending a gym after I got pregnant with Monica. I didn't want to be fat and I didn't want my partner to have a reason to leave me. I was totally convinced that my husband would leave me if I gained weight; I was pregnant and I wasn't fun to be around me anymore. Somehow, this was the sort of motivation that kept me going to the gym while I was carrying a baby.

On one occasion, I went to the gym and I was doing cardio. I saw these beautiful little ladies in bikinis lifting behind my trainer, the owner of Gold's Gym. I looked at them and then to myself. I was almost nine months pregnant, huge, and walking on the treadmill so slowly.

After I finished my 45 minute treadmill session, I went over to the owner. I said, "Mike, when I deliver my baby, I want to look just like them." He looked at me and asked who, and I answered, "Just like those chicks that you're training. I want to look just like them." he looked at me like, *"Yeah, yeah, sure. Right."* And then said, "Come see me after you have the baby."

Monica was a little drama princess from the very beginning. Even when she was inside my belly, she caused chaos. At 20 weeks, I was rushed to the emergency room because I couldn't breathe. I had been coughing for a while, and it turned into something worse. The doctor diagnosed me with asthma. I had to use an inhaler for the rest of the pregnancy.

They had me at the hospital for a whole week. It felt like forever, the doctors were afraid that my little baby was not getting enough oxygen from me and that as a result, she could even die.

She was also a breech baby. The doctors had already tried to turn her by hand when I was 36 weeks. This procedure is called external cephalic version (ECV). However, she was very stubborn! They tried for an hour, but as soon as they had her properly turned around, she would flip back to the breech position—she wouldn't move. After that, the doctors decided a C-section would be performed at 40 weeks.

On a Monday morning, I started having contractions a week prior to the scheduled C-section, so I drove myself to the hospital. They admitted me, and Monica was born at3:30pm. A healthy six pounds, 20-inch baby.

Monica is six years old now, and she emulates me and everything I do. I guess I'm a living example for her. We go to the gym and she just sits there and watches what I do. Sometimes she even tries to lift up five pounds. "Mommy, I want to be like you. I want to eat healthy so I can have muscles like you, Mom," she says. She likes to come with me to the gym. She likes to go shopping with me. She likes to go to Victoria's Secret. It is her favorite store and when we are in there, she wants to get eye shadows, lipsticks, absolutely everything. She is a mini diva, my little girl. I call her THE princess because she's not a princess, she's THE princess.

And she is so funny. One day I was fixing her bed and I burped. "You can't burp in front of a princess, Mom," she said surprisingly. And it seems that I can't burp in my house anymore, not in front of my princess, because in a way, she has to live up to the example. I need to be very aware of the example I'm giving to my little girl. Like any other mother in the world.

The bond between us is so strong. I never felt the same with my adopted daughter, Katherine. I loved her very much, but it is a different kind of love. There is definitely nothing like the bond between a mother and her child. It is such a strong thing, watching her is like watching me. She shares my characteristics, my personality, she is my little rebel. She is just like me and when I look at her, I see her as my creation. Now that I have my son and my daughter, I feel complete, utterly complete.

After everything I have been through with the pregnancy, when I look into Monica's eyes, I know the journey to get here was really worth it.

# *Fitness*

Going back in time to two weeks after I'd delivered Monica, I showed up at the gym and I looked for the owner. I said, "Mark, I'm here. Remember me? You told me to find you after I gave birth."

He looked at me and said, "Okay. How can I help you?"

I said, "I delivered my baby. I'm here. I want you to train me."

He said, "Was this a natural birth?"

"No, it was a C-section. She was a breech."

"No," he said. "You go back home and come back in a month and a half."

I looked at him and I said, "No. You told me that you were going to train me so I can look like those ladies. I want to look like them. You either train me, or I'm going to train myself."

He said he saw such a determination in my eyes that he agreed to my demand. So he said, "Hell, I have to train this chick, otherwise she's going to kill herself."

From that day on, I got into fitness big time. I wanted to inspire and be an example for those women who think, "Oh, I'm too old for this. I have children now, I have no time to work out." In the Hispanic culture, one statement I heard a lot is "I got pregnant, and now I have to eat double." The preconceived idea is that you have to eat twice, for the baby and for you. That is not true. That's not what I did. While I was pregnant, I kept working out and making healthy choices to eat. My pregnancy didn't slow me down, even though I was experiencing a living hell. I was still working, eating healthy, and training, until the very day I delivered my baby!

But that is what I want to let people know, especially women. You can do it! I did it, you can do it too. That's the mindset that you need to be in. Not just like, "Okay. I am going to change my eating habits for one day so I can lose weight for a week," or something like that. That's a crash diet. That's not a lifestyle. You have to change your whole lifestyle. You have to be healthy and start eating healthy and show your children. Lead by example. They need to get inspired by something, by somebody. I want to help motivate them.

Ten months later, after giving birth, I was in the best shape of my life! I competed in my first body building show in Panama City Beach in 2010. I placed 4th and received a medal. Three months later, I competed again in Orlando. Right before this competition, my father passed away. It was very emotional and difficult time for me, but I competed as hard as I could to dedicate it to him, my beloved father.

In March 2012, I was in North Carolina doing heavy deep squats. I was weightlifting for an upcoming competition in April, I put 425 pounds on the bar. With the last repetition, I didn't get the right posture and paid for it. I heard a crack in my lower back and the pain was unbearable; I dropped the weight and the pain went all the way to my toes. I thought I was paralyzed; that I was going to be handicapped for the rest of my life. My newfound passion would be gone; my new success out of the door.

Eventually, I just hoped that it was a sprained muscle. I ended up competing anyway, despite the pain.

I decided to see the doctor after the competition was over. As I walked the stage in my high heels and greased-up body looking hot enough to burn down a house, I smiled through the pain. It was good enough for me. I didn't place, but I looked good and did the best I could with the pain I was having.

I finally went to see the doctor the following Monday. He sent me to have an urgent MRI on my back the same day. That night at 8pm, I received a phone call, "I got your MRI results." the doctor told me. "How are you doing with the pain? What is your level of pain?" I told him I was lying down, and that it was very painful, but was okay. I was dealing with it.

Then he told me, "Your L4, L5 and S1 are crushed. The best comparison that I can make is to an Oreo cookie, if the white substance in the middle has been squished out. The liquid between the disks in your spine is like the filling in an Oreo cookie and is gushing out as the discs are being crushed. You're going to need to see a neuro surgeon."

I started crying, "No running. No exercise."

He said he could give me the names of some expert doctors in the field, but eventually, I decided to do my own research and asked my trainer at the gym. He referred me to a good sports medicine surgeon and assured me that he would turn to surgery only as a last resort. I followed his advice, got an appointment with this extraordinary doctor, and asked him if there were any options besides surgery.

"Sure," he said. "We can try physical therapy and steroid shots in your back."

We tried the steroids and they didn't work; it was sickening. I happened to be allergic to the steroids and I got rashes all over my body. I gained weight and started to hold water, and even broke out and got pimples everywhere. I looked terrible. It did not take the inflammation away and I couldn't do absolutely anything with my life. I was left in a state worse than before.

I had been doing physical therapy for about three months. It didn't work. I still was in pain. My right leg and toes kept going numb. It was getting even worse than before. The doctor told me that I had nerve damage on my right leg. He said, "Well, the steroids didn't work, and neither did the physical therapy. I guess we will have to cut."

*But can I still work out, do squats? Can I wear heels?* I thought he was going to place metal rods down my back.

I asked what that procedure would be like. He says, "A lumbar discectomy is a procedure where we will repair the bulging or herniated (vertebral) disc in your spine. A laminectomy is performed first to gain access to the injured portion of the disc. Then the outer wall and soft center of the injured disc that is bulged or herniated can be removed relieving pressure on affected nerves."

He sent me to a nerve specialist, who confirmed that the most damage was in my right thigh.

"You need the surgery," he said.

I only wanted to go through the procedure as a last resort, but nothing else was working. I wasn't feeling any better, and had lost almost all feeling in my leg. During all of this, I was still undergoing physical therapy. They were prescribing me morphine every day, but I did not want to take it. I just didn't want it because I'm allergic to painkillers. All of it was devastating; I wasn't competing in any body building, and all my energy was toward getting my health together. During the last two years, competing in fitness competitions and maintaining a healthy lifestyle was keeping me alive. I thought all my medical problems were behind me. I had more energy and I was really soaring to new heights. I was on the way to success and all these new health issues were getting on the way.

Finally, we scheduled the surgery. My doctor told me, "It's very simple. We're not going to put rods in your back. We see how much damage there is, and if it's not a lot, then you'll be good to go. Any complications and we'll keep you. It's easy. You'll be okay."

The first time I went for the surgery, they told me they couldn't operate because I was taking Adipex, a weight loss pill that depletes your heart of an enzyme it needs. I had gained so much weight because of the steroids that the doctors had prescribed me the Adipex.

I had to suffer through two more weeks of pain. I was eating like crazy because I'd had the steroid shots but no Adipex. Finally, I was able to have surgery. They did a partial discectomy. They didn't remove the whole disc, just half and the other part was shaved. They said, "Come back in a week so that we can follow up with you." They also said no lifting. "Don't carry or lift anything more than five pounds."

"Great." I thought. "So I'm handicapped. I can't do anything."

The first day I got home from the surgery, I was left at home by myself with my daughter. Monica was just two and a half years old. I thought, "How am I going to carry my baby girl upstairs?" I was living in a three-story house and my bedroom was on the second floor. I wasn't willing to sleep on the couch either, it was so uncomfortable and I was in so much pain. I decided not to follow the orders of the doctor and ended up grabbing her and walking upstairs.

That same day, I went into the training room in my house where I had my cardio machines and did an hour of walking on the treadmill. Slowly, but surely. Working out was my way of dealing with the pain. When it comes to my body, I always try to do something positive to balance it out.

Thankfully, my back healed and I was able to get into lifting again full-time.

# *The Break In*

About 10 months after my back surgery, I started to work out at the gym again. It was a Friday night and my husband, who was traveling, wasn't at home that day. I got back home from the gym and put my baby girl to sleep. I was tired and decided to take a shower. I walked into the bathroom and, as I was taking a shower, I heard the house alarm system state, "Garage door open". I thought, *It can't be my husband, I just talked to him on the phone. He's in Washington and there's no way he can come back home this quickly. Someone is in the house and it isn't him.*

He'd trained me well and placed several rifles and pistols around the house in case someone ever broke into the house. As a matter of fact, he'd had placed an AR-15 under my bed. Without a second thought, I jumped out of the shower, naked and dripping water, grabbed the rifle from under the bed and placed it around my waist. I didn't think twice about it, my survivor's instincts immediately kicked in. It is 11 at night, this person is not going to come in and say, "Hello Miro, how are you?" It was about surviving and defending my child and myself.

I was terrified, holding all 15 pounds of equipment and called my husband, telling him nervously, "Someone is in the house!"

"Do you have the rifle? Grab the rifle, Miro!" he said.

"I have the rifle, I already have it!" I answered.

He was getting more worried by the second, "Call 911!" I put him on hold and called, hoping for them to answer my call right away. As I was on the phone and walking to the hall, I heard footsteps, as if someone was rubbing himself against the wall. The adrenalin kicked in. I remember looking down the hall, placing myself in front of my daughter's bedroom and screaming at the top of my lungs, "I have a gun and I'm not afraid to use it! I'm going to blow your head off!" I lit up the laser and started to scan around in search of whoever had broken into my house. Suddenly, I heard footsteps again that seemed to be getting further away and I could hear clearly the door close.

"You have a rifle!" said a voice on the phone. I had completely forgotten I'd called 911.

"Yes, I was going to use it," I said defiantly.

Eventually, the SWAT team came over and asked me what had happened. "I was in the shower and I heard the garage door open. I grabbed the rifle and walked into to the hallway. I was not going to let him go. I knew this person wasn't going to greet me nicely." I replied.

"Wait a minute, you got out of the shower. You were nude and holding a rifle?" the officer smirked.

"Yes, sir," I replied, dead serious. He was surprised to hear that I wasn't wearing any clothes. I was completely naked with a rifle in my hands. I guess it was more like a scene from a movie.

They assumed the thief had cloned the garage door opener and that was how he had got access into the house. A patrol car stayed outside the house for the remainder of the night, even though I felt like I didn't need it.

Two days later, I came home after work to be greeted with another surprise. Around 6pm, I was in the bathroom again when I heard the front door open, which set off the alarm that announces, "Front door open". I always close the door, and I knew I had locked it with the deadbolt and chain. For a second, the idea of someone cloning the door key crossed my mind.

I grabbed the rifle again, ready to take on anyone who was coming through that door, and ran downstairs to find that the intruder had left again. When I opened the front door, I could only see a red truck and heard the screeching tires. I called 911 again and the guy on the phone said, "Okay, is he gone now?" After I said he was, he said, "Put your rifle away, young lady, we're coming."

I asked the deputy to dust for fingerprints. After examining them the police told me a few days later that the only fingerprints found were those of the previous owner of the house. Maybe he'd left something valuable in the house and was coming to pick it up. Who knows?

I'm tempted to think that the first intruder was someone who knew about the painkillers we had in the house. Someone probably wanted to steal them and sell it on the streets. But nobody got away with anything in my house! I will always protect my family, no matter what.

# *Liver*

The following October, I was in a car accident. It was a year after my back surgery and exactly one day after my last appointment with the doctor. "It's been a year, you are good to go, Miro. You don't have any more issues. I don't want to see you back here." The doctor smiled.

It was the day after the good news when I got involved in an accident and hit my head on the wheel. It basically shook my brain and caused me to lose consciousness. Soon after, I had to start taking medication because I was having problems with my memory. I was having amnesia again; it was hard for me to remember the event, where and how it happened. The person who'd hit me was texting and driving, and when he hit my car from the back, everything went black.

The next thing I remember was being in the parking lot of a car rental place. Somebody knocked on my door and told me something. I don't remember what, but then I blacked out again, and then the next thing I saw was a beautiful lady. I had never seen her before, she had long brown hair and was in a white dress, knocking on the window.

"Do you need anything?" she asked. "Are you okay? Do you need anything? Do you need water? I could get you some water."

I said I was fine, and she asked me if I'd called 911 yet, and I said no. She walked in front of the car. I saw her walking, and then she disappeared into nothing.

Eventually, I was taken to the ER. I had a CAT scan, and they saw that there was no bleeding in my brain. They released me and diagnosed me with a concussion. They prescribed me more painkillers and muscle relaxers, which I didn't take. I'm very stubborn because the problem was more about the nuisance of having to deal with the itching and feeling of not being able to breathe since I'm allergic to the painkillers. I had to take a Benadryl instead for the reaction, and it knocked me out and dealt with the pain.

Soon after, my eyes started to get yellowish. So my doctor sent me to the gastroenterologist. He said my liver enzymes were high. The ALT enzyme is typically around a 50 count, mine was almost 200! The other enzyme AST should 30 and mine was over 100. This means there was some capsular inflammation. They did a CAT scan and found some weird spots on my liver.

My doctor sent me to have a biopsy on liver to see what was going on. After the biopsy, I couldn't breathe. I couldn't laugh. I couldn't giggle. I didn't really know what the problem was. So, I just sucked it up like always, and went on with my life.

Three days after I got the biopsy, I was checking my social media pages and felt like I had hunger pains. Then I thought maybe I had an ulcer. It was hurting way too much to be hunger. I realized the pain was from my liver, not my stomach. I got really cold, and then I fainted. Eventually, the paramedics were called. My blood pressure was high: 225 over 120. I was shaking, cold, and sweating. When I was in the ambulance, I started vomiting blood. That's when I knew things were getting serious.

When we got to the ER, I was throwing up and had a blue bag in my hands to puke in. I was so weak that I dropped it and a female doctor came over and said, "Do not vomit on the floor because there are more patients that have to be seen in a place like this."

I looked up at her and motioned her with my finger to come closer to me. When she did, I told her, "Where do you want me to puke? In your face?!" The doctor looked at me completely surprised and I told her, "Get out of my room now, and send me another doctor!"

She thought I was a drug addict for how sick I looked. I was spacing in and out and asking for morphine to keep the pain away. "We are not going to give you anything because we don't know what is going on."

I was hopeless. I begged them, "Please give me something for the pain. I need something for the pain!"

They gave me Phenergan to stop the vomiting and sent me to get another CAT scan. Immediately after the scan, the technician grabbed the doctor and they wheeled me into the OR.

In the operating room, a bunch of doctors entered. They had to do an embolization of the liver which consisted of a catheter tube inserted in the femoral artery that goes to the liver. Through that incision, they placed the apparatus that stopped the bleeding of my liver.

The liver is a blood bank, and I was bleeding to death. I had no idea. They finally starting pumping morphine into me and I started to feel better. They needed to keep me awake though, because breathing moves the liver up and down.

The procedure took about three hours in the operation room because it was very difficult to put the apparatus on my liver the right way.

Apparently, when I previously had the biopsy done to inspect the liver spots, the technician did it in the wrong part of my liver and way too deep. After they got the bleeding stopped, they administered more morphine and the doctors sent me to the ICU as I wasn't allowed to move for few days until the incision was completely healed. They said, "If you move, the apparatus in your artery could come out and you will bleed to death."

Later, a friend of mine that came to see me and said that I had looked like I was dying. Everybody thought and assumed that I was dying because of how many machines I was hooked up to.

I was in the ICU for seven days.

My enzymes were still high and they didn't know why; the doctors couldn't find out if it was cancer. They didn't know what was going on, and they didn't want to

do any more biopsies on me or start new treatments. I
didn't want to undergo any other procedure with them
either.

They eventually sent me to a liver transplant
specialist in Jacksonville at the Mayo Clinic. I had
another CAT scan done before I was sent there. I saw a
series of white spots on the images and the hematoma
due to the liver biopsy. I remembered crying and calling
my mom to tell her that I thought I might have liver
cancer.

My mom just broke down. She said, "God is great.
He's going to heal you. You know, just go to the
specialist and see. There are so many people praying for
you. Thousands of people will be praying for you, Miro."

Two weeks later, I went to the see the specialist.
He is the best liver specialist in the world. He said that I
needed an MRI, mainly on my liver, to see if we could
find what was wrong in there. I was also sent to the
blood lab. I was told they would need to draw 14 tubes
of blood to get the analysis done.

The next morning, I went for my lab tests, and to
talk to the specialist again. After they drew so much
blood from me, they had to wheel me out because I was
so weak.

At around 11 that morning, I went back to see the
doctor and it was then that I found out miracles do

happen and exist. No growth or specks were found on the MRI, my enzymes were a little high, but not in the thousands. I had no idea what happened.

"For now," the doctor said. "The liver has essentially healed itself.

At that moment, I felt very close to God. Yet, I knew that it was not my time to go yet. There must be a reason why I'm still alive. A reason why I'm still here. And I plan to stick around till I find it.

# *Today's Blessings*

I have been living in Florida since 2005. I am a full-time Family Advocate/case worker for both a private and government organization. I can't be more specific about the details of my job because of the confidentially and privacy issues that are involved. However, I can say that I help families who are in need. People that may be dealing with violent or tragic life situations. Every day, these people touch my heart. I can teach them that it doesn't matter what life throws at you, you will survive. You can get through this. I am there to hold their hands and show them the way.

Since a few angels have touched my life and gently nudged me down the right path, now it's my turn to give back. It's my turn to be an angel for someone else. To show them that there is a light at the end of the tunnel. You just have to keep believing.

I have attained a Bachelor's and Master's and Degree in Science from the University of Maryland. Despite all the hardships to get myself an education, I cannot emphasize enough how important gaining a higher education is to the quality of your life.

On top of being a full-time caseworker, I'm also a certified personal trainer and model. I've been photographed in glamour, bikini, beauty, fitness, and action shoots.

Everything started picking up for me recently. I'm really shy, I don't like to talk in public unless it's in Spanish because I'm afraid everyone is going to make fun of my accent. I was really afraid to step out of my box, but not anymore. I feel more confident than ever.

I created my website www.thelittleamazonian.com and Facebook fan page, and it went from 1 to 500 fans in just a few hours! Then it went up to a 1,000; then 5,000; then 10,000; and more and more each day. It was amazing! So many people, especially Hispanic people, loved it. They love my personal brand and what I represent for them—a strong female survivor.

I was also featured in several magazines, and was the double-page spread in a bikini magazine. I plan to publish my own bikini magazine. Although I'm still working to accomplish this goal, I believe it will be finished by the end of this year. I've been featured in *Tactical MilSim Magazine*, and part of my life story has been published there as well.

Recently I was interviewed by the "Guns, Love and Freedom Show" in Arizona. It was an hour interview about the break in to my house, why I support the second amendment and the reason why I choose to use a rifle to defend my home.

I did a two-hour interview by (WINN) World Integrity News Network in Arizona to talk about females with guns, to support the second amendment, and encourage women to protect themselves. I show them how to not be afraid of guns and to be a survivor, not a victim of violence.

I was invited by a very close friend of mine to promote some knives with my signature engraved on them. When I was there, I was approached by one of the main radio stations in Texas and asked for an interview to promote my book.

My custom signature rifle inspired by me and created by Tactical Arms of Texas will is available on my website.

I'm a great supporter of veterans and law enforcement agents. I'm a proud gun owner and patriot. I have a certificate in Firearms Training and Safety. I collaborate with organizations that help veterans, especially with PTSD awareness.

It's now 2015, and everything seems to be taking off this year for me. It is an amazing feeling. I'm so blessed. I know my success will soon turn into a financial support system for my children and their future. I know God is going to bless me. He already has.

My brain tumor from the cashew tree is completely gone. I think it has a lot to do to some natural supplements and drinks that I started taking back in 2009, suggested by my partner back then. Inexplicably, six months after been taking them, I went to see my neurologist and the rest of the growth had completely gone. Today, I haven't had any more issues. I still see a neurologist once a year just to be sure, but nothing has change. I thank God every day for that.

Unfortunately, my second marriage didn't survive. I'm still hoping to find my soulmate, but wish health and happiness to both the fathers of our beautiful children.

Life definitely isn't easy. Sometimes its darkness takes over and you may believe it won't get better. But I'm here to tell you that it will. I've survived the jungles of Panama, the wildernesses of love, and been the subject to other's evils. I wouldn't change my journey for the world, because it made me who I am today...

I AM A MOTHER

I AM A SURVIVOR

I AM THE LITTLE AMAZONIAN!

*Miroslava Espinosa*

# *About the Author*

Miroslava is a mother and a daughter. After growing up in the jungle, Miroslava moved to Japan, then settled in America. She earned her Master's Degree in Science for Human Resource Management from the University of Maryland. Today, she works as a Certified Personal Trainer, Social Worker, and Family Advocate, as well as a bikini and fitness model. She's an amateur figure body builder and an author.

To contact her for public appearances, please visit her website: http://www.thelittleamazonian.com/

View of the Chagres River from my farm

High School Graduation 1996

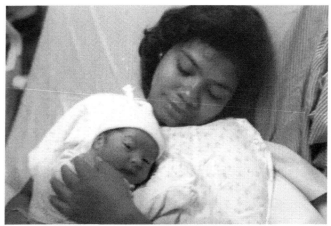

Birth of my son Christopher in Okinawa. October 1999

Citizenship Ceremony, Hawaii 2002

Bridge of the Americas 1992.

My daughter Katherine and me at her first communion

My oldest brother, his children, and me at the farm

Me at my high school graduation ceremony

Me at a friend's house 1991

Signing the buttstocks of my custom signature rifles 2015.

Getting ready to shoot my signature rifle at the range.

At the gym training for a 2012 fitness competition

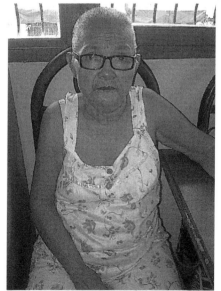

My mom at 72 years old!

The Entrepreneur's Publisher